My prayers
for all of 1

love you uall.

Shattered by Nancy Kassing

SUICIDE

Shawna Mortel

PRACTICAL STRATEGIES FOR
PICKING UP THE PIECES
AFTER THE DEATH OF A LOVED ONE

Shattered by
SUICIDE

SHAWNA MERTEL

LIFEWISE BOOKS

SHATTERED BY SUICIDE

Practical Strategies for Picking Up the Pieces After the Death of a Loved One
SHAWNA MERTEL

Published by:

LIFEWISE BOOKS

PO BOX 1072
Pinehurst, TX 77362
LifeWiseBooks.com

To contact the author | shawnamertel.com

DISCLAIMER:
This book is not intended to provide medical advice or to take the place of medical advice and treatment from your personal physician. Readers are advised to consult their own doctors or other qualified health professionals regarding the treatment of their medical problems. Neither the publisher nor the authors take any responsibility for any possible consequences from any treatment, action, or application of medicine, supplement, herb, or preparation to any person reading or following the information in this book. If readers are taking prescription medications, they should consult with their physicians and not take themselves off medicines to start supplementation without the proper supervision of a physician.

This book is designed to provide information and motivation to its reader. It is sold with the understanding that the author is not engaged to render any type of psychological, legal, or any other kind of professional advice. No warranties or guarantees are expressed or implied by the author. Neither the publisher nor the author shall be liable for any physical, psychological, emotional, financial, or commercial damages, including, but not limited to, special, incidental, consequential or other damages. Our views and rights are the same: You are responsible for your own choices, actions, and results.

ISBN (Print): 978-1-947279-88-9
ISBN (Ebook): 978-1-947279-89-6

dedication

To my three loving children—Jordan, Celeste, and Michael Jr., who inspire me to live my best life.

special thanks

To my tribe, especially Nancy Kassing, who sat beside me patiently teaching, typing, and sometimes just crying with me as I wrote this book.

To Charity Bradshaw—my coach and encourager.

CONTENTS

INTRODUCTION

On Wednesday night, February 12, 2014, I found my husband's body in our home after he took his life with an assault rifle. Without warning, my life changed forever. I honestly and passionately share my story with you so you can better understand where my desire to heal came from as well as my passion to help others find healing.

In this book, I will take you through the first year after my husband's death and the healing journey that took place alongside the stages of grief. We will even look at some of his history that I later learned probably contributed to him taking his life.

Maybe for you, it wasn't your spouse. Whether it was your child, parent, friend, or partner, the pain, shock, and grief run deep. This book is for anyone who has ever felt the shattering effects of a loved one's suicide.

If you are close with someone who has been affected by a loved one's suicide, I applaud you for being an amazing friend by working to gain insight and empathy as well as practical ways to help them as they heal.

At the end of most chapters is a section called, 'What Helped' where you will find practical things to do (or not do) and insight that helped me. Knowing what not to do can be very valuable.

By buying this book and reading even to this point, you have already taken a great step towards healing. I want to thank you for allowing me to be a part of your journey.

MY WHY

After my husband's suicide, I went through a few books on grief and suicide looking for answers to the question, "What in the world should I do?" While I found lots of information, I could not find a book to coach me through the utter shattering I experienced. This book is my "why."

I have stood, (or rather laid flat on the ground, perhaps where you are right now), wondering if the gut-wrenching pain would ever go away. I had no idea how the pieces of my life could ever be put back together. I could not comprehend how I could ever feel joy again. What I did know from previous experiences I had to work through is that if I committed to the healing process, hope and joy would return. But this shattering seemed to shake my very core. Even though it was difficult to just take my next breath, I knew I had to commit to healing. Hope, joy, and love did return and they will return for you too.

chapter one

SHINING LIGHT

FACING MY OWN DEMONS

I was raised by loving, godly parents. Their hearts were huge. My first memory in life was around the age of three. I had not learned healthy boundaries or how to trust. While trying to reach out to help a relative, I was sexually abused by this person. I was threatened not to say a word. I remained quiet and stuffed my pain and confusion. Around age ten, I became anorexic. I found that starving myself was a way to numb out all my emotional feelings, while pretending I was happy on the outside.

By the age of twelve or thirteen, my parents took me to a doctor because they were concerned about my lack of healthy fat and my diet. Since my parents wanted me to eat more, I then turned to bulimia to deal with and numb out all emotions.

If I had told my parents, they could have gotten me the help I needed. Because I never told them, or another adult, I struggled in my younger years with trust and accepting healthy love. I did not feel lovable and continuously tried to earn love and approval. I can't remember a time in my young life when I did not feel shame and guilt. I want you to understand that I know the pain that comes from not healing a life shattering tragedy right away. I was only a child and the threat of telling my parents was all too real to me at that time.

After high school, I attended Baylor University in Texas. In the fall of my second semester, a close friend from high school committed suicide. I drove to Arkansas from Texas to attend the funeral. My emotions were so numbed out, I did not shed one tear. That did not mean my pain was not great. I knew how to stuff my pain into an eating disorder and paste a smile on my face.

I initially studied science and was headed for physical therapy or medical school. After my friend's suicide, I changed my degree to psychology. I wanted to help others and maybe subconsciously try to figure out how to fix myself. Studying about healing emotional wounds and healing them are two very different things. I went on to make many poor choices out of my unhealed pain.

In 1990, I transferred to Sam Houston State University, and graduated with honors with a Bachelor of Science in Psychology and a minor in Philosophy. After graduation, I worked in Houston, Texas as a coach to help others who had eating problems. Ironically, as I helped others, my eating disorder continued to advance.

I learned I could not give what I did not have, and I did not have healing.

In 1994, I moved to Portland, Oregon and worked in a nursing home planning therapeutic activity for the residents. I took additional courses specializing in geriatrics and social work and was promoted into the social service department as the Director. Studying as much as I could on social work and seniors, I got my health insurance license, specializing in Medicare. I worked closely with the director of the facility as we added a unit for dementia patients. One particular part of my position I found especially valuable was training the nursing staff on behavior modifications as I worked with the medical professionals to prescribe less psychotropic drugs.

In 1996, I continued my passion as Director of Social Services, but also consulted in nursing homes wanting to add a secured Alzheimer's wing to their facility. I taught and trained other social workers how to obtain financial coverage for a patient needing skilled care or additional medical services.

In October 1997, Oregon legalized physician-assisted suicide. Many people living in California and Washington states that had been diagnosed with HIV or AIDS moved to the Portland, Oregon area. I started a meal program with a few nurses I worked with. We would take sandwiches to those living on the streets in Oregon. Because I was responsible for all the discharge planning, I knew many places in Portland that worked with AIDS patients. I was able to help many find a clean place to stay and receive good healthcare.

DIE OR HEAL

> Burying yourself in work or constant activities and stuffing your pain inside will only make life harder.

With the massive hours I worked, the stress and my eating disorder finally took their toll. At 28-years-old, my heart physically gave out. I ended up in a hospital and was told I was probably going to die. Fortunately, my heart miraculously healed and I no longer needed acute, in-patient hospitalization. This event certainly got my attention. I sought help for my body, mind, and soul at a center for eating disorders.

I received appropriate care which allowed my heart and physical body to heal. I also received intense therapy to unlearn all the unhealthy patterns I had developed to cope with life. I had to go all the way back to the sexual abuse at age three when I first started numbing my emotions. I started to learn how to trust, accept love and forgiveness.

As part of my treatment at the center, I was not allowed to restrict my food intake or throw up what I had eaten. This left me without a way to numb my emotions, similar to a drug rehabilitation center removing all of an addict's drugs. I was like a child experiencing life and emotions for the first time. Everything felt raw and all-consuming. I was given tools to deal with pain, anger, grief and trauma that helped me heal my deep wounds. Few people are taught these tools, even if they are fortunate enough to have a trauma-free childhood.

WHERE MY WORK BEGAN

I was at this center for nine months. Once I returned to the real world, I wanted to share what I was taught with others. I knew the pain of not addressing trauma and tragedy right away. The overwhelming pain doesn't magically go away. I learned the hard way. The transformation I experienced from this work birthed a passion and desire in me to help others who had also gone through tragedy.

In 2000, I moved to Kansas City, Missouri. I realized I needed the support of my family and moved closer to them. Around 2004, I was able to fulfill one of my dreams by coaching victims of rape or incest. I did not charge any fees and I did not advertise, but word of the results these people experienced spread quickly. Appointments for women with eating disorders, people who cut themselves, even children where traditional counseling didn't work started filling my schedule. Eventually, I had to limit how many people I saw.

People were finding joy and healing in three to ten sessions as I taught them the keys I had learned. I had personally been in traditional counseling off and on for over twelve years and never found healing until I went to the eating disorder center for nine months. I continued coaching and helping others until 2014, when my world shattered.

WHO WAS MIKE MERTEL?

Mike was from Buffalo, New York, and part of a very hard-working family. His father worked for General Motors (GM) as a union mechanic to make a better life for him and his family in the suburbs. His mother stayed home to raise Mike and his younger brother.

During his early life and elementary years, he was aggressively, physically and verbally abused by his mother. She beat him, once with a broom as he desperately tried to hide under his bed. While being hit, pushed and shoved, his mother would tell him he was stupid and would never amount to anything. She spoke many mean and hateful things over him during those critical developmental years.

When Mike was about twelve, his mother started attending AA meetings. She wanted to raise her children better than she was raised. She worked very hard to become sober. Over time, she became a good mother and got very involved in her children's activities.

As Mike grew up, he blocked out his early years of abuse by focusing on sports, friends, and school. During his senior year, he was even named the "friendliest" member of his class. He was a state champion in wrestling and excelled in football.

His dad had never even taken a sick day until the day he collapsed on the floor at GM. He was taken to the hospital where he was ultimately diagnosed with cancer and died within six months. Although very sick, Mike's dad was able to attend Mike's graduation from college, and see him commissioned as a Second Lieutenant in the U.S. Army.

VISIBLE SUCCESS, INVISIBLE WOUNDS

Mike wanted to live a completely different life than the one he knew growing up. He was the first person in his entire extended family to attend and graduate from university. He was also the first to serve in the military as an officer.

> What he never fully learned was you can leave
> your physical surroundings, get an education,
> and even excel in many areas of life but
> trauma and inner wounds that are stuffed
> down and ignored do not disappear.

I compare it to a deep cut on the skin. We can ignore it for a while, even try to cover it up but until it is completely cleaned out, it won't heal properly. The longer the delay, the more difficult the healing process.

Mike excelled at everything he put his hand to. His college years were no exception.

1986 – attended University of New York at Fredonia on a ROTC scholarship.

1987, 1988 – earned the 'Leadership Excellence' award at the Ranger Challenge.

1989 – received 'Camp All-American' during a ROTC advance camp training in Fort Bragg, N.C. 1990 – graduated with a finance degree and was commissioned as a Second Lieutenant.

Mike's commanding presence and leadership abilities propelled him to receive special assignments while serving in the Army. In 1992, while serving in Korea, the tank division he commanded earned 'Top Tank Crew'. While serving in Korea, Mike took a vacation to Phuket. He met a young woman from England who was also there on vacation. They fell in love and married several months later. She moved to America and in 1995, they had a son named Jordan.

Later, Mike served as a General's aid with the United Nations Logistics Support Command in Somalia directly after the Battle of Mogadishu (more commonly known as 'Black Hawk Down'). His desire to succeed eventually led him to the warfront in Somalia.

After returning from Somalia in 1995, Mike wanted to focus on fatherhood so he retired as a Captain in the Army. Still unwilling to deal with his past trauma, Mike's marriage ended when Jordan was only about eighteen months old. His ex-wife moved back to England so she could have help from her family in raising Jordan. Mike prioritized his relationship with Jordan and visited him in England several times a year.

THE MAN OF MY DREAMS

I met Mike in the late 1990's in Seattle when Jordan was almost three years old. I had only been out of in-patient treatment a few months. Mike was so charismatic and in charge, he seemed to capture the attention of the whole room when he entered. He was the man of my dreams.

We fell in love, but still had our ups and downs. I realized he had some anger issues from childhood that needed to be dealt with professionally. I also wondered if he struggled with alcohol. There were several occasions when we were out on dates that he would drink excessively and not want to stop once he started. In these instances, he became very angry and aggressive either at me or somebody around us.

Mike's behavior in these situations was inappropriate and unprovoked. Once while we were dating, he became enraged at me because I implied something he said didn't make sense. Because he was called stupid so many times while growing up, if he thought someone was even hinting he was not smart, he would become extremely angry.

I made no connection that Mike might have been an alcoholic. I thought alcoholics drank every day and Mike didn't do that. As much as I loved him, I knew marriage would not be wise at that time. I moved back to Kansas City because I knew distance was the only thing that could keep me from staying in this unhealthy relationship.

I went to Kansas City for a week looking for a job and found one. Heartbroken, I ended the relationship with Mike when I returned from Kansas City to pack. I hoped he would get professional help, but I couldn't force it on him. Mike had to want to heal for himself.

A few months later, Mike called me crying (which I had never heard him do). He told me that about a week after I moved away, he started professional counseling to work on his childhood trauma and he wanted to get back together. I was still madly in love with him and so proud of him going to counseling. I just assumed he had worked through all his issues, like I had.

> How quickly I forgot how long I was in counseling without much success, until I actually learned some useful keys to healing.

Mike asked, "Can I look for a job in the Midwest?" with the intention of our relationship moving toward marriage.

I said, "Yes."

He got a job in medical sales and quickly moved to Kansas City. About a month after he moved, he proposed to me. I was so excited to marry the man of my dreams. I planned our wedding in three months and we were married November 25, 2000.

A FAMILY MAN

After our wedding, Jordan spent his summers with us. Despite the distance, Mike and Jordan had a very close relationship which helped me see what an incredible father he was and would be. We both wanted more children. Just five days after our first anniversary, we had our daughter, Celeste, and four years later, Michael Jr. arrived.

We lived in an upper/middle-class neighborhood where the kids had many friends to play with during the day. My primary job was raising our children, but I also worked alongside Mike in our business doing marketing. At the time, I also coached women and children that had been sexually abused. I just wanted to see people healed from their past and present pain.

Mike and I were both very involved in raising our children. He loved spending time with me and the kids. He truly loved us. Because we owned our own business, we were able to work our schedules around our lives and children. I was able to have more time at home and Mike arranged his schedule so he could attend events, help coach sports, and participate in family dinners. He helped the kids with their homework and tucked them into bed at night. I thought we had a wonderful life, until…

NO ONE SAW IT COMING

Mike was an upbeat guy. He was never diagnosed with depression and had never threatened suicide. We were not having marital problems; although, we had worked through quite a few of them years before. I knew he loved me. He was an amazing dad, and loved his kids with all his heart. Financially, I thought things were great. I didn't see any of this coming.

Late January 2014 – Mike and I went to Cancun on a trip he earned through the company he did business with.

February 8th – the four of us enjoyed a hockey game with my daughter's Girl Scout troop.

February 11th – Mike volunteered at the kids' elementary school.

February 12th – I found my husband dead from a gunshot to the head.

———————

Mike and I were married thirteen years when he took his life. My world, and the worlds of our three children, shattered. At that time, Jordan was about to turn nineteen and was still living in London with his mom and step-dad. Celeste was twelve (6th grade), and Michael Jr. was eight (2nd grade). I needed to heal, and also needed to help our three children heal.

THE CLAY JAR

When Michael Jr. was ten years old, he attended an amazing summer camp designed specifically for children who had lost a parent or close loved one. One of the activities from camp was very significant to us—the clay jar.

When I picked Michael up after his camp was over, he showed me what he made while he was there. It was a simple clay jar, yet I saw cracks where it had been broken and glued back together to reform the jar. Expecting to see a work of art from my ten-year-old boy, I asked him to tell me more about it. His big, blue eyes got even bigger with excitement as he shared.

He told me he was given a perfectly new clay jar. The camp counselor told him to throw the jar down on the ground. He threw it down two times without the jar breaking. On the third time, it shattered into pieces. The camp counselor explained that this is how it can feel when you lose somebody that you truly love. The next instruction was to use clear glue to put all the pieces back together. The counselor explained that Michael would remain himself and continue to love his daddy just as the jar would remain a clay jar despite the broken, shattered pieces.

THROUGH THE CRACKS

Michael needed to be pieced back together and that would take time, counseling, and working through his grief. I was fascinated with Michael's story about the clay jar. When we got home, I took Michael into his room where he had a bed fort that got very dark when the curtains closed. I got Michael's clay jar, a battery-operated candle light, and we went into his fort and closed the curtains.

I put the tiny light in the center of the clay jar and showed Michael. This once ugly, shattered jar was now beautiful. Every place where the shattered pieces of the jar had been glued back together allowed light to shine through the cracks. It was now more beautiful than before it was shattered. I sat with my son in his bed admiring the rays of light. I told Michael that we can and should be a light in this world.

> If we allow healing to come, light will shine out of every place we have been broken and shattered.

I want you to understand two very important things:
1. Broken pieces of our lives need to be replaced through healing and mending just as the jar needed to be put back together to remain a jar.
2. Unless we choose to heal, life will replace those pieces with unhealthy things.

We each must do the work of healing. Grieving is not always fun, but it is necessary. I shared with Michael how he had started with just an ordinary clay jar, but now his clay jar had become a masterpiece. I explained to him that he was also becoming a masterpiece. We were each designed to be beautiful masterpieces by our Creator.

As I share my journey of healing with you, you will see the cracks, some of which are quite large where light can shine its brightest. Life is about putting the shattered pieces back together. Just like the clay jar, once broken, you will never be exactly the same; however, you can heal. Hope and joy can return to your life, and you will be able to shine through your cracks. An intact clay jar can only shine light from its opening, but a masterpiece shines light out of every point of reconnection and healing.

(In the back of this book I've included some information about grief camps available to teenagers, children and even families that are free of charge or cost very little.)

CHILDREN AND GRIEF

If you are responsible for children, you must heal yourself *and* help them heal. I know that is an extraordinarily difficult thing—to help someone else heal and grieve when every breath hurts and all you want to do is hide away from the world. You can do it! Working on your own grief will help your children know it is alright to grieve and important to work through your pain. You are your children's role model for how to grieve.

Don't be fooled. If you have children, they might look fine on the outside despite a deeper struggle. They need to be equipped with the tools to be healthy on the inside. The child's age at the time of the tragedy will often be the mental age that child gets locked into as they grow and mature. (Assuming the child was mentally healthy for their age beforehand.) Children often stuff their emotions. They may appear healthy until adulthood, and then, "out of the blue" that adult child can no longer deal with life in a healthy way.

A child might act out by getting into trouble at school or other unhealthy actions as they try to deal with their pain. Teenagers might become unmanageable and rebellious, or start using drugs to numb the pain and hurt. For adult children, grief that wasn't dealt with will often manifest itself and result in depression, alcoholism, drug abuse, outbursts of anger, and/or issues with developing stable relationships in the future.

Neither you nor your children will magically wake up one day and be healed. Regardless of their age, they need appropriate healing tools at numerous stages as they grow and mature. They will not forget or just move past their loss, even if they aren't talking about it.

Healing from a loved one's death is never easy and takes time, especially death by suicide. You may feel like you will never be the person you were before the tragedy. Even if somehow the pieces of your life could be put back together, it may seem like joy will be gone forever. Know that each broken piece of your life can heal and light can shine through the cracks brighter than before. My heart's desire is that you understand the importance of doing the work of healing so you can live with hope and peace.

WHAT HELPED

Time does not heal! You must actively pursue healing from grief.

Replace the word "suicide" with "took his/her own life". "Suicide" brings to mind such violent acts that I find it difficult to use the word about someone I loved so dearly, especially when I'm talking to my children about their daddy. No one is disputing the fact that suicide is a horrible and violent act against one's self. Whatever you decide, make sure you are comfortable saying it. I promise as soon as someone finds out your loved one died, the very next questions will be, "How? What happened? Why?"

Life is worth living. Understand you have been through a life-altering tragedy. Life has forever changed. Healing, hope, and peace will seem more like an impossible dream rather than an attainable reality. You might even start believing the LIE that life is just too difficult (a lie that I heard over and over in my head). Please, please hear me: YOUR life **is** worth living!

You are priceless! You have a great destiny to fulfill and so do your loved ones. If you are having these thoughts, call the 'National Suicide Prevention Lifeline: 1-800-273-8255. Let someone close to you know what you are thinking as well as tell a counselor or professional. I absolutely did not want to take my life, or leave my children without a parent, however, in my head I loudly heard, *"Your life is over. You might as well die"*, etc. I entered into a 'Suicide Prevention Contract' with my counselor for fifty days.

By 9 am each morning, I called my counselor and I told her, "Today, I will not hurt myself on purpose or by accident." If my counselor had not heard from me by 10 am, she would call me. If she could not reach me, my signed contract gave her permission to send the police. This is just an example of what a 'Suicide Prevention Contract' might include.

Also, get rid of any guns or pills you might be tempted to use to take your life. (Remember, this is only temporary.) Also, please know these thoughts are very common when you have lost a loved one by suicide.

'Survivor's Guilt' is a real thing. It is often experienced when a loved one dies before their expected time. Children also experience Survivor's Guilt, depending on their age and ability to understand death. At twelve, my daughter blamed herself for her daddy's death for almost a year. My son started to blame himself around age eleven—three years later!

(Appendix B goes through the developmental stages of children dealing with grief. If you have children, this appendix will be a valuable tool for you to better understand what your children can mentally understand about death. In chapter three's 'What Helped' section, we look at Survivor's Guilt in much more depth.)

Keep two journals. In the first journal, write the new ways you are learning to heal. This journal will be like an emotional toolbox where the tools will be the things you find helpful as you move through grieving. When you read something you want to remember, write it down. As you hear something good from a counselor or grief group, write it down. Be committed to doing the work of grieving so you can heal. Trust me, it's worth it! Plus, if you are also helping children through grief, you might want to add a special "Kid's Section" in your journal.

There will be days that you grieve more than others or when the gut-wrenching pain feels stronger than ever. Remember, that doesn't mean you failed, and it does not mean you are not healing. Do not get lost in your grief or stuck in what has shattered you. You can heal! This is when you pull out your journal and look through your tools. Keep trying until you find something that helps you feel better. Later, add that to your journal.

In the second journal, write about new things. If you do something for the first time, write about it. Don't downplay your achievement! For me, paying the bills was a "first" for me. Yes, I should have been already helping with them, but I needed to celebrate that I was doing them now. We cannot live in what we 'should have', 'could have', or 'would have' done. We must live out of our 'today'. My journal is filled with things, from buying my first vehicle to repairing a toilet.

Start right where you are. If you are reading this and thinking, "I have already blown it", or "I did not do that for myself, my kids, or friends and family", IT IS OKAY! You are right where you are supposed to be. Forgive yourself. Remember, no one does this grieving thing perfectly. If you hear otherwise, the person sharing is not telling the truth. Grieving is not a one size fits all process. Each individual goes through it differently.

Although often referred to as 'steps', grieving is not that simple of a process. The loss of a loved one is grieved in different stages for those who mourn. It is the hurt that is shared. Grieving is an ongoing process in which there is no perfect plan. Those steps in grief are not ones that we can simply check off as done. We greet each day with its unique issues and move forward. If you missed the opportunity to deal with something in a healthy manner, just wait. You will get a second, third, and fourth chance to get it right.

Be aware of grief reactions and habits. Two years after Mike's death, I discovered a list of common reactions. I wish I had it earlier. That is why I have included it in this book. After reading the list, I realized I was 'deep sighing'. I thought I was anxious or out of breath all the time. Once I realized it was a common reaction to grief, I was able to catch myself as I started to sigh and take a slow breath in. Knowledge is power; just knowing I wasn't going crazy helped me stop that behavior.

Michael Jr. started habitually putting his hands up around his mouth and he ended up with rashes in the area. One of the ways we addressed this was by putting a rubber band around his wrist and every time his hand went towards his mouth he would snap the rubber band. The main thing is to be consistent, especially if you are working on one of your behaviors. It took about three months to stop his behavior.

(Appendix A addresses, "Common Ways People React During Grief".)

Sleep is necessary and important as well as preparing for sleep. I wish I had been told *how* to sleep better. As soon as my regular physician heard that Mike took his life and I had found his lifeless body, she called in a prescription of sleeping pills that I had taken in the past. Even with a prescription, I could not get more than two hours of sleep the first week. The second week, I remember getting three hours of sleep a couple nights. The pills did not help much.

(Please, do not take prescriptions written for anyone other than yourself.)

Here are the things I've found to be very helpful prior to bedtime:

- *Write down your 'To Do' list before bed.* This helps your mind keep from focusing on everything you need to do the next day and allows for better rest.
- *Avoid alcohol, and caffeine after 3pm.*
- *Shut down all electronics/screens at least two hours before bed.* Neuroscientists believe blue light from screens negatively affects health and sleep patterns.[1]
- *Ask your doctor about vitamins and supplements to help support your health.* Two supplements I started taking at night that helped were; Adrenal Calm, by Maximized Living, and 100 mg of magnesium citrate. Consult your doctor before taking any vitamins or supplements.
- *Use specific essential oils in diffusers.* Wow, I had no idea how helpful essential oils could be. I put diffusers in all our bedrooms. Lavender has been a great aid for sleeping, as well as oils blended to help with peace and calming.

(For more information on essential oils, I have included some information in the back of the book.)

Make no big decisions for at least one year such as moving or a job change. This was a very good piece of advice I received. If you are able to do that, fantastic. If not, I would seek the advice of at least three trusted people, including one that specializes in the field of the decision you must make.

I was in shock for three to four months. I attended meetings, signed paperwork, and months later had no memory of them. Luckily, these meetings did not include big decisions.

Close all joint accounts as soon as arrangements can be made. I learned this the hard way, which is why I encourage you to address this as soon as possible. Mike had credit cards he had maxed out set up on automatic monthly payments through our joint checking. I was not aware of these credit cards nor were they in my name. (I should have participated in paying the bills, but that is a whole other story) Upon finding out Mike was dead (about a week after), the credit card companies began withdrawing the monthly payments repeatedly until every penny was gone.

One well-known credit card company withdrew the monthly payment three times in one day! I had no idea this was even legal. At the very least, make sure you stop all automatic payments until you can get a handle on what bills are coming in and funds going out.

chapter two

THE LONGEST NIGHT OF MY LIFE

Mike did not plan on taking his life that day, but looking back I think he must have considered it an option. Mike had never threatened suicide; it was so out of character for him. During an argument a few years earlier, he mentioned that the kids and I would be better off with his life insurance money than him. I quickly told him that was a lie. He never mentioned anything similar again. Mike knew about my friend from high school that committed suicide and how difficult it was on me even though I had not seen her in over a year because of college.

THE PERFECT STORM

Little did I know when I woke up on February 12, 2014, that the longest night of my life was hours away and that I would not sleep again for days. I had been sick since we returned home from Cancun. I didn't take care of myself and the cold turned into a sinus infection by the time I finally went to a doctor. Mike was very thoughtful and picked up my prescription on his way home from work. He had also bought pizza for the kids to have for dinner.

When he arrived home from the pharmacy he had one of the kids bring me my antibiotics. Had he brought them to me himself, I would have immediately known he had been drinking. From upstairs in my bed, I could hear Mike laughing with the kids when suddenly I heard his tone of voice change abruptly to irritation.

I knew something was up because his mood didn't usually change that fast and he didn't normally get irritated with the kids so quickly. He was usually consistent, and controlled his anger when disciplining our children. I got up and went downstairs to see what was wrong. As soon as I saw Mike, I knew he was drunk.

It was Wednesday night and our daughter wanted to go to church youth group. From what I observed, he was upset because he was way too drunk to drive. At that time, as far as I knew, Mike had not drunk alcohol in two years.

FROM ALL WALKS OF LIFE

When Michael Jr. was eighteen months old, Mike and I hit rock bottom in our marriage or so I thought. That was when I understood he had a problem that alcohol exacerbated. I had never been around alcoholics and just assumed they drank every day and couldn't really hold down a good job. I soon realized alcoholics come from all walks of life.

Mike was successful, not only in business and with people, but also as a dad, and husband. He was a godly man with many friends. Mike drank every three to six months—so how could he be an alcoholic? But when he drank, he couldn't stop. He would drink until he passed out. He was usually a nice drunk unless he was questioned, then he got angry. Then, the two to three days after a drunken episode, he would not act like himself.

After about seven years, that anger turned scary and I was no longer willing to live that way. The anger appeared the day after the drinking binge and lasted one to three days. We started seeing a counselor and he even found a church where he could be honest with the preacher and some men there. Prior to moving churches, I did not feel comfortable talking about his anger and drinking problem. Once we made these changes, things improved and Mike only drank one to two times a year.

A MAN WITHOUT A PLAN

But on February 12, 2014, everything was different, especially how drunk he was. He got up from the couch as I came downstairs from my bedroom. He told me he was going to take Celeste to youth. As he got close to the front door to leave, he fell down. He was a big man at six foot four. I had seen him drink a lot but I had never seen him fall-down drunk.

I took his keys so he would not drive anywhere. I did not feel safe and my gut told me to get both kids and leave the house immediately. I told my kids to go to the garage, get into the van and wait for me there.

This was the last time my kids ever saw their daddy.

Since I had been in bed sick and still in pajamas, I had to change clothes before I could take the kids to church. I had already told Mike several times in our past that if he ever drove one of our children when he had been drinking, we would separate until he got help for his problem. When I came downstairs, I told him I couldn't believe he was going to drive our daughter to church when he was so drunk to which he yelled, "Don't you judge me!"

I did not want to engage with him because I was too afraid. I said, "I love you and we will talk tomorrow when you're sober." As I drove the kids to church, they asked why I was taking them instead of daddy. I told them their father had been drinking and we were going to say a prayer for him. There wasn't a class for Michael Jr. and me at church that night so we worked on Valentine's Day cards for his class at school instead.

SOMETHING'S NOT RIGHT

While driving home from church, an ambulance passed us. Even though it was going a different direction, I felt something was very wrong. As we drove in the driveway to our house, I commented how odd it was that our cat, Jack, was sitting in the front window. Normally, he would be lying on Mike, especially if he was passed out. We walked into the house and it was quiet, so we all started yelling and looking for Mike. No answer. I went to the basement and the kids looked on the main floor then headed up to the second floor. As I heard them take the stairs, I got a sick feeling in my stomach and ran up to the second floor after them.

Celeste said he wasn't in her bedroom. As she came towards my room, I saw a large hand imprint on her chest gently pushing her out of my room. (*This was a miracle because there was only glass separating her from the scene. I know an angel was with her covering her eyes and gently pushing her out of my room.)*

After I saw that imprint, I told both kids to go to their rooms and I ran into mine and shut the door behind me. In our jacuzzi tub, I saw a huge assault rifle lying on the body of the man I loved, the man I was going to spend the rest of my life with, the daddy to our kids. I went into shock.

(I have never described exactly what I saw to anyone and don't want anyone visualizing that horror.)

ADMITTING IT OUT LOUD

Making sure I shut my bedroom door, I ran to my children. Even in shock, my spirit reminded me to have my kids get their favorite stuffed animals and comfort blankets. I led them outside and across the street to my neighbor's house, told them to call 911, and that there had been a terrible accident and their daddy was hurt. I was also on my cell phone with 911.

My neighbor came over immediately after making sure the kids were with her daughter, a close friend of Celeste. She had them play in the back of the house so they would not see all the emergency vehicles. I could hear myself telling 911 to hurry with an ambulance. I was outside hitting my head on the front step covered with ice repeating, *"Where is the ambulance?!"*

My neighbor wanted to go up to check on Mike, but deep down I knew what I saw, and I knew Mike was dead. I told her not to go because I did not want her to have that image burned in her head. I finally admitted out loud that Mike was dead.

I knew God healed. I knew He even brought people back from the dead, so I decided I had to go back to my bathroom and pray that God would bring Mike back. If my children ever asked me if I prayed for God to bring their daddy back from the dead, I had to be able to tell them, "Yes I did." Not doing it would go against what I had always said I believed and more importantly what I knew God was able to do. I held his cold hand and prayed like I had never prayed before.

> I soon felt it was time to stop praying
> because Mike had, with his freewill, made
> the choice to take his own life.

THE IMMEDIATE AFTERMATH

I went back outside with my neighbor to wait for help to arrive. It felt like a million years before anyone showed up. Police came, many police, but never an ambulance. I think some firemen came. Even a priest showed up.

Once the police finally left and the coroner had taken Mike away, I sat across the street in my neighbor's house feeling totally numb and lost. It was all too surreal to wrap my mind around. I knew, in the depths of my soul that God was good, but this nightmare wasn't. Nothing made sense. My pastors were out of town, but thankfully two leaders from my church had already shown up.

I remember I was told it was getting very late, and that I needed to tell my children. *TELL MY CHILDREN?* How could I tell them their loving, wonderful daddy was dead? He wasn't depressed, (that we were aware of). He had just brought pizza home for dinner and was laughing with them only hours before. Even though I had said he was dead once, I still hoped something supernatural or super crazy would happen and Mike would walk through the door. I didn't want this nightmare to become real.

The next thing I knew, I was sitting with my kids. I told them God was good but we live in a world where bad things can happen. I told them there had been a bad accident, and daddy was dead. Michael (8) began to cry and Celeste (12) sat in shock. One of the leaders helped me gather some things for the kids and myself to spend the night with the other leader and her family. I have no idea how we got to her house. They thoughtfully gave their master bedroom to me and the kids so we could hold each other.

DIFFICULT PHONE CALLS

I still had to tell Jordan (18) but did not want to tell him over the phone without telling his mom first. They were very difficult to reach in England with a six-hour time difference. Thankfully, through social media connections, we reached his mom around 3 AM. I told her what happened. I wanted her to be there to comfort Jordan, and trusted she would know how much information to tell Jordan if he asked more questions.

I love Jordan as my own child and it hurt beyond measure to tell him his dad who had loved him with all his heart was dead. At eighteen, Jordan was told his daddy had committed suicide while in a country where nobody really knew or loved his dad. He was able to make it to Kansas City about three days later where he joined those of us who were also mourning.

At about 4 AM, I received a call from Organ Donor Associations wanting to harvest his organs. I was utterly confused and had flashbacks of Mike's condition wondering what could they use. I consented. They were actually able to use more than I imagined.

A SPECIAL MIRACLE

While I was still awake, I looked desperately at my cell phone for any message from Mike. Somehow, despite my technology challenges, I found a place on my cell that had deleted messages. Suddenly six to eight messages from five months earlier appeared even though months of messages had been deleted.

Mike left me these voice messages when he and his brother volunteered at a conference in North Carolina. Miraculously, I was able to retrieve these precious messages. They were all amazing inspirations of his love for God and for his family. He was having encounters with God and seeing miraculous signs and wonders. Every call ended with him telling me he wished I was with him and how much he loved me. I played them over and over.

GOOD AT HIDING

I know taking his own life wasn't something Mike thought out because there was no note. But in that intoxicated moment, he believed the lie in his head that we would somehow be better off without him. Such a lie! Sometimes our loved ones are good at hiding the deep pain they are experiencing and sometimes we are just too close to see it. This is important to understand because as survivors, we can easily slip into guilt.

Survivor's guilt is a real thing. My children and I, and even Mike's mom, all experienced it for a time. *"If only I had done this or that differently, I could have somehow stopped the suicide."*

Please know, in a tragedy such as a suicide, there is NOTHING you could have done or you would have done it. Of course, we would have done anything, but we didn't know. Stop assigning fault on yourself. Say out loud, "It is NOT my fault".

If you, or a child you are raising found your loved one, please go to the doctor and get examined for shock or post-traumatic stress disorder (PTSD). If untreated, shock can turn into PTSD. In Chapter 4's What Helped, there is greater detail on a therapy that has been used to treat people that have gone through traumatic events.

Familiarize yourself with the ten stages of grief. It's easy to feel like you have lost your mind or are going crazy when you don't know that it is actually normal when grieving. These stages are listed in Appendix A.

Pay attention to what's triggering your grief reactions. If you recognize that you are reacting to grief in one of the ways listed in Appendix A, I would encourage you to write it down in your journal. Write down what is going on before you react. This will help you notice if there are specific people, places, or events that might be triggering your reaction. As you gather more information, you will be able to decide on one or two ideas to replace the current way you are reacting.

There are some situations you might need to avoid for the moment. Your grief counselor can also help give you some suggestions.

Beware of "emotional blackmail". Over the last several months, I've read remarks from people who've lost someone to suicide and a common theme appeared. The deceased told their loved one they "could not live without them" or "would die without them." This is called 'emotional blackmail' and it is intended to manipulate the other person into not enforcing their healthy boundaries or consequences of bad behaviors.

Some had caught their loved one returning to addictive drugs and behavior and had asked them to leave until they got help for that addiction or behavior. Instead of getting the much-needed help, their loved one chose to take their life. If this sounds like your scenario, know it was not your choice, and is NOT your fault.

Talk about your loved one. I know that by the time you are reading this book, you have already been shattered and have probably already had your longest night. I wish I could take away your pain, but I will say it does help to surround yourself with people that love you. Talk about your loved one, what they did that was funny or cute. Share stories of fun times and remember the great times you shared. Share those silly things you thought you would never miss. For example, I missed stubbing my toes on his giant shoes that he left in the middle of the room.

You can control the dialogue. There is a temptation to try to explain why your loved one took their own life. "Why?" is typically the first question a person will ask. People are curious and they've heard rumors by now. It's human nature. We are often drawn to the ugliest of life and relieved when it wasn't our tragedy.

So, deal with the questions as humbly as you can. Remember most people do care, are probably shocked, and just want to try to understand. You and I both know if we had answers, our world would probably not be shattered right now.

One strategy that helped tremendously was writing out the most troubling or disturbing questions people were asking me. I then talked to a trusted friend and counselor on how I could respond. She told me to say, "My counsellor has asked me not to discuss that when I'm not in counseling. Sorry." Then I would ask them if they would share a nice or funny story about Mike. This shifted the focus off their inappropriate questions and moved the topic to something more positive. I rehearsed my answers and even wrote them on notecards. If the person continued asking rude or difficult questions, I would pull out my note card and read directly from it.

Allow others to help you with everything. The good thing about being shattered is everyone knows. No sense pretending you have it all together even if you are telling yourself you should. It is in our greatest times of need and weakness that we find bonds with those around us. Nobody has it all together. Swallow your pride, allow people to clean for you, help with your children, bring food, or hand you tissues.

Have a designated person who can be responsible to write down who did what or gave you what. My mom was very good at writing those things down for me, but I wish I had gone one step further. Because I was in shock, and as embarrassing as it is to say, many 'thank you notes' were not written. Years later, some stuff has still not been returned. Find someone who will sit down with you and write those thank you notes and maybe even return some of those dishes for you.

I remember when I wrote a thank you note to my neighbor across the street who was with me from the beginning. How could I put into words what she had done to help me and my children? It took me over two hours to write that one note and I could hardly see what I wrote through my tears. Also, please have someone open every card you receive. Two years after the funeral, I finally opened a card from Mike's old business partner and his wife. Inside the card was a check for two hundred dollars. Not only did they never receive a thank you, but WOW, I sure could have used that money (and of course a check over two years old is no longer good).

TWO POINTS OF CAUTION WHEN RECEIVING HELP:

First, ask your helpers to not wash any of your loved one's clothes unless they have shown them to you. I desperately wanted to smell the scent of my husband one last time, but everything had been washed.

Secondly, I would make sure friends helping to clean don't throw away something that might have been special to you and your loved one. I felt so violated after the biohazard team came into my house and threw away over thirty large trash bags of my things. *(This is explained more in the next chapter.)* Even with friends who were helping, I did not understand why I was so upset every time they threw something away. I knew how much they were helping me. Please know that this is a normal response to overwhelming loss. It's like someone who lost their home in a fire; you just want to hold on to everything that survived the fire even if it is trash. Maybe that piece of trash has handwriting on it, or a picture. I recommend telling your helpers that you are having a difficult time.

Prepare in advance how you will respond to comments and others' tragic stories. People will say rude, hateful, or even mean things often without realizing how hurtful their remarks can be. Give them grace, but don't allow them to hurt you further. Prepare a generic response that will work for those unexpected moments. Many people tried to share details of 'their' tragedy (which was usually some long-lost cousin, uncle, or friend of a friend) that had taken their life. If they didn't have a personal story, they would share the latest suicide seen on the news. I would pull out my note card, interrupt their story and say, 'My counselor has instructed me not to listen to stories that might bring up flashbacks, or terrible memories. I would love to hear a happy memory of Mike, if you would like to share one." If the person was somebody I wasn't probably going to see on a regular basis, I would simply say, "I can't listen to this, sorry."

Be prepared to repeat yourself. When I say, "Give them grace", I mean there are people who try to relate to you by sharing something similar. What they just don't understand is that your situation can not be improved by hearing another tragic story. Their experience is not the same as yours and won't help.

RESPONSES FOR THE CHILDREN

Children need responses, too. What should a child say when asked about their deceased parent or when others are talking about it? It can be very challenging for a child when their friends are telling stories (even good ones) about the deceased parent. They need a plan of action.

I would recommend you and your child talk to a grief counselor for ways to help them answer tough questions like: *Where's your dad? How did he die?* One thing I taught my kids to say when someone at school asked was, "It is personal to me and my family" or "I don't feel like talking about it right now but thanks for asking." I asked my kids questions and we practiced their responses. As for questions from strangers, I taught my children to just say, "You need to ask my mom", or "I'm sure you are curious, but it is personal to me and my family."

Your kids will need practice and that is normal.

Stay in continuous communication with your children about what they are hearing or being asked. Shattering tragedy does not usually happen in private. When Mike took his life, the whole neighborhood knew and at times, it felt like the whole world knew. Your children will be asked many questions from people who too often just want the gross details. Remind your children they do not have to answer anything! They don't know 'why' any more than you do. They have been through too much and don't have to deal with insensitive and rude questions.

chapter three

JUST SURVIVING

THE NEXT DAY

Ice still covered the ground, but somehow the sun rose on February 13, 2014. Most of America would be celebrating love the next day, February 14th. The nightmare I was living was not just a bad dream, it was real. Very real. Mike was dead.

I was in psychological shock, which I did not realize. Even though an ambulance had come to my house the night before, I was never examined by any medical personnel. What I now know is when someone is experiencing shock, they can be confused with an extreme inability to concentrate.[1] I recommend seeing a doctor if you witnessed such an event or found your deceased loved one.

I did not put the pieces together until a year later when I was sitting in a school meeting with my daughter's teachers. They showed me paperwork I had signed just months after Mike's death. I had no memory of the meeting I had attended to sign paperwork related to my daughter's first year in middle school. Seeing my signature a year later, I realized I must have been in shock.

On February 13th, I told Celeste her daddy had taken his own life. I could only explain there had been a horrible accident and he was dead. I did tell her how at that time. She did not cry. She just stood there in shock and confusion. I desperately wanted her to know how much her daddy loved her. From the day she was born, she was the light of his life. I wanted all my kids to know that.

The friend we stayed with told me that Celeste was continuing to ask what had happened to her daddy. I knew I should be the one to tell her before somebody else did. I thought my heart would burst out of my chest. I was hurting so much, gut-wrenching pain that was so deep I really don't have words to describe the agony I was going through.

CLEANING AND CLEARING

My parents must have jumped in their car as soon as they were told because they arrived at my house from Arkansas by midafternoon. This is normally a nine to ten-hour drive. They picked me up and took me back to my house while the kids remained with our friends. A respected friend, who had come to the house the night before, met us there. He informed me that I needed a biohazard team to clean up and take care of the master bathroom and everything else that might have been affected.

When a tragedy, such as a suicide, occurs inside a home, it can leave behind a heaviness in the atmosphere. The first thing I did to change that atmosphere was to play positive, uplifting music in the bathroom and throughout the house. I kept music playing twenty-four hours a day for the next few months.

By the second night, our pastors (who were close friends and lived in our neighborhood) arrived back in town and my children and I stayed with them. Again, that night, we all stayed in the same room. I read to them from the Bible until they fell asleep. I prayed over them all night since I could not sleep.

> I could barely close my eyes because, when I did, the horrific scene flashed across my mind.

I kept my children away from our house the next few days while the biohazard team worked. I did not want them to see the level of destruction and debris being removed from the house. A huge Jacuzzi, a wall, and over thirty huge, yellow biohazard bags filled with contaminated items were removed. I had black trash bags placed over the fireplace and over the glass bathroom door. Now, none of us could see into the bathroom.

BEING ROBBED

Everything not shut in a cabinet or closet had to be removed and destroyed. Unfortunately, most of my toiletries and makeup were sitting on the bathroom counter. To give you an idea of the devastation, it was twenty-three feet from his head to the back of the closet and the closet door had been left open. Because of the stringent nature of the biohazard team, everything within that twenty-three-foot radius was removed and destroyed. I didn't even have access to the clothes that were in my closet.

Bags and bags of clothes, shoes, other things from the closet, makeup and toiletries were just gone. The Jacuzzi and a large section of the wall had to be removed. The carpet and pad were removed and the base floor was scrubbed. Even the ceiling had to be scraped and scrubbed.

I had no idea what I had or did not have at this point. For the next few years, I would be looking for a specific outfit or necklace and realize it must have been thrown away by the biohazard team. The closest thing I can relate this experience to is being robbed. I felt personally violated each time I realized something else I once treasured was gone, thrown out with the trash. Yet I also felt shattered. Unfortunately, I settled with the insurance company long before I knew the full extent of what had been removed.

IN THE DARK

When Mike died, I knew nothing about our personal or business finances. Mike took care of all of that. I didn't even know where to start. Mike had done much of our banking online. Of course, in addition to not being very familiar with computers, I did not know any of Mike's online banking codes and passwords. I was completely locked out of every account.

Mike and I had a business together. He had all the licenses and did the primary work and selling while I did the calls and all the marketing. Our company was over without Mike. On February 12th, I lost my husband, and on February 13th, I lost our business and all means of financial support. Everything seemed shattered into a million pieces. How could our lives ever be put back together?

My dad spent hours going through Mike's office at our house attempting to sort through all the papers. He also took me to our banks where we had four accounts. I closed two of them immediately. I remember being at one of the banks with my dad to close an account. There I sat with the bank manager and my dad; I was crying so hard I couldn't talk. I could barely breathe. Since he felt there was no time like the present, the bank manager decided this would be a good time to inform me that the huge accidental death policy we held through that bank would absolutely not pay out.

Mike always told me when he got a sale and how much money we made. What he did not tell me was when we lost money. I thought we were doing alright, financially. I learned that zero is not as low as a bank will allow your balance to go. In fact, one credit card company had withdrawn $300 dollars three times by the time I got to the bank to close that account.

Mike took pride in taking good care of us and being the financial leader of our home. He had gotten us into some financial trouble, the full extent of which I would not discover for months to come. Two weeks before Mike took his life, he shared with me through tears that he had an argument with his mother. He had had a close relationship with her. He was very ashamed that he had been charging business expenses on a credit card his mother had generously given him to use only in emergencies.

When she saw the huge balance, she was rightfully upset and had the credit card cancelled. Their last conversation was the day after Christmas, when his mom yelled things at Mike she used to say when he was just a defenseless child. Mike was being reminded of deep wounds he had long since buried. He was capable of earning enough to pay the credit card off in just a few months but looking back, I think those wounds and his pride prevented him from seeing clearly.

Now, I learned money was owed to everyone, everywhere. I did not know that Mike had not been working for at least three months and had been charging our living expenses on different credit cards I didn't even know he had. I wish I had been more aware and involved with our finances and budget. (Rather than live in regret any further, I've learned how to budget and teach my children about money.)

I was completely in the dark.

How could we have gotten in so much financial trouble so quickly? How could I have been so blind?

Mike earned a trip just months earlier through one of the financial companies we did business with. We enjoyed that reward in January. He had made so much money over the past year, yet I was looking at a mountain of debt that I could not wrap my head around.

On February 14th, Valentine's Day, I had to plan the funeral for the love of my life, the man I thought I would spend the rest of my life with. Instead, I found myself planning his funeral on the most celebrated day of love.

MAKING ARRANGEMENTS

My mom and dad took me to the local funeral home. Until then, it was the only one I had ever noticed. Now, I notice funeral homes everywhere. The funeral home worked with me to arrange the military honors for Mike's burial, but I had to come up with the obituary to be printed in the paper. What was I going to say about my strong husband who had been the leader of our home and family? Suicide was the complete opposite of the man I knew. I wish I would have reached out to some of our friends for help, but of course, my thoughts were far from normal. Beyond the basic announcement, funeral homes charge to write obituaries. This wasn't even an option since I had no money.

At one point, I looked at the funeral director, stood up without saying a word and went into the bathroom lobby. I collapsed on the floor crying and hyperventilating. Everything felt surreal. I honestly don't remember the rest of that day. My biggest concern was making sure Jordan made it in for his daddy's funeral.

The next few days were a blur. Friends came over to clean my house, food was delivered and family was arriving from out of town. Receiving help was hard for me. I liked being the person doing for others, 'the helper'. I was not used to being the one in need. Even in the emotional process of writing this book, my close friends surprised me and came over to clean my home.

> If people offer to help, I strongly
> encourage you to say, YES.

I did ask a dear friend, Nancy, to put together a slideshow of pictures for the funeral. Her husband is a computer expert, so she took Mike's computer and cell phone to save any important information and all the photos. I wish I would have had someone go through his contacts in his phone to let them know about his death. Years later, I ran into former clients that did not know what happened and were completely shocked. We would grieve together as if he had just died.

THOUGHTFUL DETAILS

Nancy had been widowed at a young age so she could relate to much of what I was experiencing. Her help and support during this time were amazing. She suggested I have someone take pictures during the funeral and dinner that followed saying, "You might not want pictures right now, but in the future, you will wish you had some pictures to share with your kids." Another close family friend and her husband agreed to take the pictures. I am so thankful this was done. Because I was in shock, I don't remember much about who attended the visitation or funeral. The pictures help fill in those gaps.

My friends were so thoughtful. They put out blank cards at the visitation and funeral asking family and friends to write down a favorite memory of Mike. They also asked Mike's friends on social media to do the same. What a gift for me and the kids to look back on. I am most thankful for the people who took the time to write down their memories of Mike. Truly priceless.

Mike had been the leader of Michael's Cub Scout troop since Michael Jr. started scouts. I asked my dad to get in touch with them so the Cub Scouts could come to the visitation and show support for Michael Jr. They showed up in full force wearing their uniforms which was a great distraction for Michael Jr. Watching them run around gave me hope that, for at least that moment,

Michael Jr. didn't think about the fact that he would never see his daddy again.

One of Celeste's friends took her shopping and bought her an outfit to wear. Michael Jr. wore his dress blues from Cub Scouts. Even by the day of the funeral, I still didn't have full access to my closet. Being in shock does not remove what every southern raised girl knows—you must wear black to a funeral. I went to my basement bedroom and grabbed the only black dress in that closet. It was a long black formal dress a woman might wear to a party, not a funeral. I didn't even remember what I wore until much later that year when I saw a picture. I am so glad I can laugh about that now.

Before the funeral started, Stan and Leslie Johnson arrived from Texas. As soon as I saw them walk into the funeral home, I burst into tears. I did not know my heart could hurt more than it already was. Stan had baptized Mike in his own home, and had been instrumental in helping Mike learn the Bible. Mike loved them with all his heart, and so do I. Stan graciously spoke at the funeral.

CINDERELLA

One thing that Mike and I always said with pride was that we wanted Celeste to dance at our funerals. (Of course, we were planning on them being many years in the future after we were old and gray.) This started when Celeste was only about four years old. After dinner, Mike and I would turn our chairs away from the table to watch her dance. When 'their song' *"Cinderella"* came on, Mike would get up from the table and dance with her. He would twirl her around and sometimes she would stand on his feet.

> I knew Mike would want his little
> princess to dance at his funeral.

I asked five men to dance with Celeste. I also asked them to stand in the gap as male figures in her life in the years that would follow. Lee, who had been with us from the first night, ushered Celeste from the table and walked her to the front to meet her Papa, (my dad), and they started dancing to the music. As the song played, four more men stepped in to dance with her; Jordan (her older brother), George (who we stayed with the first night and who later became my children's godfather), Austen (a cousin she felt closest to), and Uncle Steve (Mike's brother). When the music stopped, they escorted her back to her seat.

A very good friend of Mike's from high school posted this on Mike's Facebook page:

> "His wish was to have his little princess, Celeste, who is a dancer to dance at his funeral! There was not a dry eye when she danced by his side with five amazing men in her life to the song *Cinderella*. From brother to uncles to cousin and grandpa all vowing to guide her through life as Mike Mertel would have!"

Mike's favorite song, *"I Can Only Imagine"* by Mercy Me was played during the funeral. If you are not familiar with the song, here are the lyrics to the second verse:

> "Surrounded by Your glory,
> What will my heart feel?

Will I dance for you Jesus,
Or in awe of You be still?

"Will I stand in your presence,
Or to my knees will I fall?
Will I sing hallelujah?
Will I be able to speak at all?
I can only imagine."[2]

When the first note was played, I heard in my spirit as loudly as if someone was whispering into my ear, *"Today you will worship Me on your face!"* So, in my ridiculous black formal, I got on the ground, face-first and worshiped my God. I did not care what I looked like, and I did not care what people thought of me. I knew in that moment that everything within me had to obey what I had just heard. For the first time, I also felt in my heart that Mike was in God's presence. I have since been told that some of my friends thought I was on the ground hyperventilating again, or having a mental breakdown. Either guess would seem plausible.

I don't remember much during his service. However, I do remember my flag presentation and worrying if a flag was going to be presented to Jordan. Apparently, according to pictures, I was standing while the Military played *'Taps'* and fired the gun salute. The gunshots threw me into horrific flashbacks of seeing Mike dead. I almost fell down, but thankfully someone caught me. Just like a salute, different events or conversation in everyday life can bring back those tragic and horrifying memories.

A dinner was served following the service. I had always been one of the main people decorating for holidays and special events. I remember walking in for the lunch and seeing the tables beautifully decorated like I would have wanted them. I was blessed to be surrounded by so many loving friends and family who took the time to do something simple but so meaningful.

ANGER AND GRIEF

The funeral was over and family started to leave. Mike's mother and brother had been staying with my dear friend across the street. Mike's mother had not spoken to Mike since their argument at Christmas. I can't imagine her pain and hurt. The debt left on her credit card seemed to be her main focus, probably for two reasons:

- Anger is a mask that hides deep pain, and
- She had no measurable means to pay off her credit card.

Some people use anger to fuel them to action, while grieving can be disabling. Not healthy, but often done.

> It didn't change that my children needed the love of their grandma now more than ever. And I did too.

The day after the funeral, Mike's mother had to fly home. All I can remember about her being in town was how angry she was at Mike, me, and our children. The only conversation I recall having with her was completely focused on her telling me I needed to pay off what Mike had charged on her credit card. I couldn't think beyond where money for gas might come from much less how I would pay off her credit card. I felt like her love for me had turned to anger and rage. I felt as if I lost my mother-in-law and my children's grandma the day after I buried Mike. It was heartbreaking.

When life shatters and emotions are fragile, it is difficult to remember that others are devastated also. I had to work with my counselor on how to best communicate with my mother-in-law. See 'What Helped' for some examples.

My children continued to stay out of school the rest of that week. I really don't remember how long they stayed out of school all together. Celeste and Michael's teachers came to the house and brought a huge basket of food the kids would enjoy. They made blankets for each of the kids to snuggle. Michael's teacher brought Valentine's cards that every kid in his class had written telling him how sorry they were. I could not believe how many people were continuing to bring things to the house. Jordan was able to stay about three more weeks before he had to return to London. He had a close friend who was very supportive that stayed with us as long as Jordan was able to stay.

PILES OF PAPERWORK

Creditors were now calling on my cell phone. Clinically, I was still in shock. I could not make sense of anything, especially the mounting debt I was learning about. Sleep sounded more like a myth than an actual reality. My doctor had called in a prescription for sleeping pills for me, but even taking the prescribed amount, I wasn't sleeping more than one or two hours a night.

In the weeks following Mike's death, my parents dug through piles and piles of paperwork in Mike's office. Paul, a friend and past business partner of Mike's, offered to help my dad go through it all. Paul and my dad had insurance and financial backgrounds, so they were able to sort through the chaotic mess of papers. They were amazing. I do not think anyone else on this earth would have been able to make sense of it.

Paul also offered to put together our taxes for free. What a blessing!

Matt, a friend from our old church, was a lawyer and offered his help. We hadn't seen him in at least five years, yet his generosity was astounding. He gave my family money to help with the immediate bills. He also looked through paperwork that my dad and Paul were able to organize to see what type of legal help I would need. Legal help? I didn't realize I would need any legal help!

> No one could find my name on
> anything; it was like I didn't exist.

My name was not on the house loan or the deed. I was not on any of the house bills. Nothing! Matt informed me that I would need a probate lawyer. Matt's sister specialized in probate law and he offered to pay her to do all the pre-probate work. Basically, it meant Mike had died with no will, no joint bills, no paperwork that proved I existed, except a marriage license. The marriage license was the only proof the creditors needed to come after me. The license was not enough; however, to prove I lived in our home and used the water, gas, and electricity.

The next month, I worked through massive amounts of paperwork helping to sort through exactly what and how much would go through probate. I would take the children to school, sort through debt all day and then pick them up from school and focus on them.

Our business was gone, and so was my job. It was no longer a question of if I would have to go through probate, but when.

Three highly qualified lawyers informed me that my probate case would not only be difficult, but it would take at least eighteen months. I was facing more than six hundred thousand dollars of debt. I had no authority to sell my home (it wasn't mine). Even if I was to walk away from our house, I had no credit to qualify for any apartment in town and no money. I needed a miracle; actually, I needed many miracles. I will share the things I learned and wished I had already known, in the 'What Helped' section. But you will have to keep reading to find out if I got my miracles.

AN OUNCE OF PREVENTION

I wish I would have been more aware and involved in our finances. I can't change how things happened for our family, but hopefully, this information can help save you from some of the pain and overwhelming heartache. I know you might be in the middle or the aftermath of a loss, so this may be too late for you, but perhaps you can help bring awareness to those around you on the importance of knowing about important paperwork by taking these steps:

- Please, please make sure you are on your house loan, the deed on the house, and at least some of the house bills.
- Communicate with your partner about finances. Know where your money, bills and investments are located, along with relevant passwords.
- Make a WILL!! It seems ridiculous to write something so obvious. Mike was even a financial expert, yet he did not have a will. If a death was self-inflicted, life insurance only pays out after holding that policy for at least one year in

the state of Missouri. I believe some states require a life insurance policy to be active for at least two years. Other policies, posing as life insurance, call themselves 'Accidental Death' policy or upon death by suicide. I now have two wills: one if only I die, and another one if my children die with me.

WHAT HELPED

Start seeing a grief counselor. (Even if you don't think you need one.) DO talk about the person who died. Use their name, tell funny stories and share things they loved. In a safe counseling environment, discuss their faults, what made you feel angry or frustrated and where your relationship truly was. Talk to someone who will move you forward in the healing process. If you are unable to find someone in your area, you may contact me for additional coaching. See the back of this book for details.

Take care of your health. Easier said than done, I know. Luckily, I had just started taking antibiotics, so I had to eat twice a day to take my medicine. That helped me because just the thought of eating made me feel like throwing up. Appoint someone you trust to check in on you and make sure you are remembering to eat and that you are eating healthy. You must eat even when you don't feel like it, especially if you have children depending on you. It takes energy to heal.

Exercise. It can help release tension, anxiety, and frustration; fight depression and promote feelings of well-being. If you have children, include them in some exercise. I remember just days after Mike's death going on a walk with Michael Jr. and talking to him about his daddy. I asked Michael if he knew how much his daddy loved him. He looked at me and said, "Yes". I ask him how he knew and he said, "Because daddy told me he did right there" as Michael pointed to an empty field near our home. This opened up a whole conversation about a rocket they built and launched in that field. Exercising together can give you opportunities to talk about your loved one in a more casual setting.

Get your pain and anger out. When I was angry that Mike was no longer with me or our children, I would punch pillows. If you have access to a punching bag, use it. It is a very beneficial way to release pain and get in a great workout. I didn't, so I used pillows. Just make sure whatever you punch is soft. As I punched the pillows, I would cry out what I was feeling until I became tired. Before I stopped punching, I would yell out positive quotes and positive words from the Bible over myself. Always end your punching session with something positive.

Respect your need for time to heal and grieve. You will need to allow time to grieve your loss. I suggest picking two specific days every week and for at least one hour on those days. Allow yourself to cry and grieve. Often people forget to make space for their loss. I remember thinking, "If I allow myself to cry, I will never stop." Giving myself permission and time not only allowed for healing but also, I didn't have as many unexpected bursts of uncontrollable crying. This will assist your healing process.

Even if you don't get much time off work, make space for your loss. The temptation is to keep yourself so busy you won't have time to think about it. Trust me, this will only result in more pain and grief later and will stop your healing process.

Pay attention to your atmosphere and keep it positive. I played uplifting faith-based music in every room, especially the bathroom, (where I found Mike). That is a great way to change the atmosphere. I played my children's favorite relaxing music quietly in their bedrooms (on repeat) throughout the night. It helped them fall asleep and not have nightmares. Several apps offer free deep sleep, healing music or meditation play lists that are designed for sleep that play for four to six hours. Music is an easy way to lift your spirit and soul. I also found the use of essential oils to be extremely beneficial for me and my children.

Think about your five senses as you think of ways to positively affect your atmosphere. Some things I would suggest are: limit television, especially watching the news. I'm not suggesting you blind yourself to the world around you. I'm just saying you should read your news, and focus on the highlights versus every tragedy that has occurred around the world. Remove items from your environment that continually bring back pain. For instance, I had to get rid of some of the plants donated at the funeral. Have friends help you clean and organize your home. This will actually declutter your mind as well as your space.

Do not settle with your insurance company before you consult with informed friends or an attorney. I felt rushed to settle on an amount. The biohazard team only gave a vague description of a few items that were thrown out and I was still in clinical shock not wanting to even think about the mass quantity of things they trashed. Our insurance company paid a percentage of the item destroyed. This meant they wanted me to replace an item, send them a receipt, and then they may reimburse me. Looking back, it seems ridiculous that any company would require so much.

I went shopping with my mom a few weeks after Mike's death to try and replace some things as required. I was crying so hard, I had to pull over and have my mom drive. Please, make sure you have an encouraging friend go with you if you have to replace anything.

Take your time. I wish I would have had my lawyer talk to the insurance company for me. I ended up not replacing most of what was destroyed. I don't think I ever sent more than six receipts in for further reimbursement. I ended up losing thousands of dollars. Get help in this area. Shopping and replacing material items are the last things on the mind of someone whose life has been shattered. I get that, but please don't lose more money because doing what is necessary just seems too difficult. Appoint a trusted friend to help you. Remember, things can always be returned.

Understand, survivor's guilt is a real thing. Celeste blamed herself for her daddy's death for the first eight months. When I found out what she was thinking, her grief counselor and I were able to address the thoughts that were telling her that somehow this tragedy was her fault. Michael Jr. seemed to be healing well right after Mike's death. Then almost two years later, he became very depressed. I took him to his pediatrician thinking he might have mononucleosis because he appeared so lethargic. The doctor tested his blood and anything else she could think of testing. I hoped it would be something physical, something that could be seen and therefore treated. (Oh, how we parents want to take away our children's pain.)

Just when I thought my heart could not hurt worse, he was diagnosed with clinical depression. I increased Michael's grief counseling and started spending more time with him at night during our bed time routine. Finally, after three months of deep depression, Michael told me he blamed himself for his daddy's death. I was surprised and horrified. *How could he blame himself?* Was this 'Survivor's Guilt'? YES! At least now I could tell him the truth; it was not his fault! Appendix B, the 'Developmental Stages of Children and Grief' was huge in helping me know the healthy phases of grief for my children.

I talked with his counselor as all three of us dealt with his feeling and beliefs. Within a few weeks, Michael started feeling like his old energetic self. I share this story with you, so you can truly understand that most people deal with survivor's guilt after surviving a life-shattering tragedy. This includes children. I later learned that around ages ten to twelve, children are able to grasp the concept that a death has occurred and think it might be their fault. At eleven, Michael was right in that target range. So, parents, don't blame yourself, or think the counseling your children received has failed. Their minds are just catching up with the shock that someone they loved died much sooner than they should have.

I took both my children to their pediatric physicians. In both cases, the physicians wanted to place my children on antidepressants. They informed me that antidepressants can cause increased thoughts of suicide. Because of that risk, I decided to look for other solutions, (i.e. restart grief counseling, adjust food, use essential oils, increase exercise, monitor if what is being watched and listened to is positive and uplifting).

As a child's mind develops, their ability to understand death also develops. For more on this, refer to Appendix B: Developmental Stages of Children. Deal with these emotions and remember, IT IS NOT YOUR FAULT!

Our thoughts have power. Whether that power is negative or positive is up to us. When we keep thoughts bottled up in the dark, and the light of truth is not allowed in to dispel it, we can end up depressed, or overwhelmed. When Michael Jr. finally told me why he was so upset, His counselor and I were able to speak truth over him.

The lie buried within survivor's guilt is like a roach that wreaks havoc in the dark. In the light of truth, you are able to identify and get rid of that roach.

Create boundaries with family and friends that are grieving in a way that could be emotionally harmful to you or your children. Talking to you (or even just seeing you) might trigger feelings of loss for your loved ones that could be taken out on you. Maybe they are blaming you, or angered that you did not see 'the warning signs.' Whatever the reason, you must protect yourself (and children) from further pain caused by someone else's grief.

Surviving children are often told, 'You must not cry,' 'Be strong for your mom or dad,' or 'You are the man of the house now'. Someone actually told my eight-year-old son that he was now the protector of our family. Celeste was told not to cry, and therefore she didn't. *These are very unhealthy and damaging things to tell a child.*

Check in with your children regularly about what people are telling them. I suggest asking if anyone has said any of these common phrases to them. Make sure you tell them those words are not true and their role in the family has not changed. They are to be the child and react accordingly.

There were some people I just could not talk to because their anger was too great. I communicated with cards and special gifts that would remind them of their loved one. It's very difficult, I know. I have learned so much over the last few years that I wish I had known that first year after Mike's death. Creating boundaries is something I go into in much more depth during my personal coaching.

chapter four

CHOOSING VICTORY

NEW REALITY

Since the funeral, my long, sleepless nights turned into weeks. Jordan was only able to stay with us a couple of weeks. I had him use his dad's cell phone while he was with us. When Jordan would call me, Mike's picture would light up on my cell phone. I would get so excited thinking it was Mike calling me. I still could not fully accept the fact that Mike was not coming back and that I was not waking up from this nightmare.

This was my new reality; widowed at forty-five. I found myself with a lot of questions:

- *Would Jordan want to visit now?*
- *Michael Jr. was only in second grade; would he grow up not remembering his daddy?*

- *Would Celeste, her daddy's princess, now leave the security of elementary school and successfully start middle school without her daddy?*

Another new reality was the overwhelming $600,000.00 debt which included the house. Shortly after Mike's mom returned home, she called me from the parking lot of a lawyer's office. She was considering suing me for the money Mike charged on her credit card. Thankfully, she decided not to, but her anger and grief over losing Mike made communication with her very difficult and we haven't seen her since the funeral.

LOSS AND REJECTION

Michael Jr. had a friend who was like another son to us. He had even given Mike a nickname that all the other kids called him: "Big Mike". Over that last year, Michael's friend would come over every school morning for breakfast. Then Mike would pray over the kids and go outside to play catch with them until the school bus arrived.

On February 12, 2014, Michael's friend came over like usual and played football with Big Mike. Without warning, Big Mike was gone. This friend never came over before school again. I don't know what he was told. He and his family were at the funeral, but how can a little boy make sense of what happened? I know I couldn't.

A couple weeks later, this friend said some hurtful things to Michael out of confusion and sadness. I called his mom crying. Looking back, I wish I had not called her. I wish I had just dealt with Michael's pain. Michael lost his best friend that day. Even though his friend sincerely apologized, their friendship was never the same.

Celeste started getting bullied at school. I had to take both kids off the bus because of the horrible things being said to them. Things like, "A real man doesn't kill himself, so you'll never become a man" or "Your dad killed himself because of you." Other children refused to come into our home because it was where Mike died. Some parents would no longer allow their children to play with mine. One of my neighbors decided it was their job to inform me that my husband was in hell and I would be joining him. I had never experienced such indescribable grief in every part of my life. I wanted desperately to protect myself and my children from further loss and rejection.

I HAD A CHOICE TO MAKE

Three weeks had passed, and I was still in shock. Deep in my subconscious, I knew I had a choice on what I was going to believe. I had chosen to heal from childhood sexual abuse and no longer thought of myself as a victim. I had gone on to coach rape and incest survivors, "sharing my healing along the way." But now I felt paralyzed, so shattered I could not think beyond the pain.

> A mentor of mine had the courage to tell me, "You have to choose victory."

Now, if you have not had someone speak hope over you, I will. You must chose victory even when all the evidence around you appears to say the opposite. Often when someone makes a choice to believe life can and will get better, their emotions don't just immediately line up with that choice.

CHANGES FOR THE BETTER

The remodeling and construction crew that was hired started as soon as the biohazard company had finished around February 19, 2014. I hired them because the head of the remodeling team told me about his best friend who committed suicide recently and how he understood what I was going through. He said he would personally make sure my bathroom and closet were remodeled to look completely different and beautiful. I felt like he would honor what he said. I told him how difficult it was for me to sleep in my room with the bathroom right there. He assured me that the remodel would be his top priority. He told me it would only take four to five weeks to complete which made me feel a little relief.

I started inviting any and every minister I knew to come to my house and pray over my bathroom and the rest of my home. The atmosphere in my home started to change for the better. Miracles started piling up even more than my losses, as my attitude changed. I chose to expect great things to occur.

Three weeks had gone by and my church was hosting a conference about how to experience the Glory of God. By then, Jordan had returned to London and Celeste and Michael had returned to school. That freed me up to attend the conference during school hours.

Kevin and Cathy Basconi were leading the conference. Mike had loved Kevin's ministry and had been to Kevin's conference in September of 2013 held in North Carolina. Both Mike and I loved to help during their conference.

THE POWER OF COURAGEOUS TRUTH

This was my first time to see Kevin and his ministry team since Mike had taken his life. I did not anticipate how difficult it would be. With each old friend I ran into, the grief of seeing them without Mike by my side became too much. I ended up running to the bathroom weeping uncontrollably until I collapsed in a panic attack.

I pushed myself up off the bathroom floor so I could attend the next session. Kevin pulled me aside to talk. He did not try to comfort me like most others or tell a relatable story, which usually made me feel worse. He had the courage to speak truth in love over me. His words shifted my destiny.

Kevin acknowledged my life had been shattered and that I could easily allow my circumstances to turn me into a victim. Then he said, "Shawna, you have to decide if you are going to be a victim or be victorious." Wow, before I could get offended by what he said, the reality of his statement sank in.

Could I really have a choice? I could not change what Mike choose to do, but I could choose how I respond. You can also choose how you respond. You can choose to put the broken pieces of your life back together. Just like you decided to read this book and work towards healing.

That day, I made the choice that I would be victorious, and that my family would all be victorious. I would not allow this tragedy to define the rest of my life or my children's lives. Looking back, this was the best advice I received.

> You have to make the choice or life makes it
> for you, and life always chooses victimhood.

I choose to be a victor. I am not a victim. I will not allow my life to be chosen for me. I went home from the conference, feeling hopeful for the first time since Mike's death. I was so excited; I attended all three sessions the next day. Another night passed with only one or two hours of sleep, but I was ready for an entire day of learning.

Just because you choose victory doesn't mean life will suddenly become easier. In fact, it may feel like the universe is conspiring against you. You might have been living as a victim for so long that it has become your new 'normal' and friends and family are not comfortable with your optimistic choice.

Remember, we have to choose victory every day. This is one of those very important things I recommend you write in your journal, "Today, (the date,) I choose to live my life in victory!" I try to remember every morning before I get out of bed and before life tries to rattle me, "Today, I choose victory. Whatever happens today, I can choose how I respond."

HORRORS AND MIRACLES

When certain events beyond natural explanation occur, they're not always from heaven. Before I left my house to attend the next session, I went to get something from the back of my minivan. When my hatch lifted, I saw two clear freezer-sized zipping bags.

Inside each bag was an item of evidence and a police evidence form listing the item and where it had been collected.

One bag held a single shell casing from the bullet. The other bag held the clip from the assault rifle Mike had used to take his life. I never put this in my van! How on earth had evidence bags ended up in my family minivan? Was someone playing a cruel joke? I dropped the evidence bags to the ground in horror. I lost my breath as I looked around for who had done this terrible thing. No one was around.

Then, a miracle occurred. I remembered I could choose how I responded. I chose victory. I put the bags to the side and drove my van out of the garage. I returned inside, got my positive notecards, and took them back into the garage. I put the evidence bags on the concrete garage floor and got my hammer. I arranged my notecards with their positive sayings on the floor and read them out loud. I took the hammer and repeatedly hit the two evidence bags as I yelled, "I am victorious!" I also yelled what I had written on the notecards. I shouted anything I could remember that was positive. I shouted who I was created to be and what I was created to do. I also shouted victory over my children, my finances, and my home. It didn't matter if I even believed it yet, if it was positive, I shouted it each time I hit the evidence bag.

By the time I had exhausted myself, the bullet casing and the magazine clip from the assault rifle were unrecognizable. I fell to the concrete floor weeping. Nothing was going to take away my victory or try to steal my life, or the life of my children. I took the two white evidence reports that the police wrote and shredded them into confetti. I threw everything away so my children would not see them. I did not allow the horror of what I discovered in my van to keep me from returning to the conference. As you will read in the next chapter, I am very glad I made that decision.

You can choose to not live as a victim as well. Life can be cruel, as you have already experienced. The good news is you have a choice. Choose victory.

WHAT HELPED

Victory is a daily, conscious choice you make. The consequence of not deciding is actually choosing to live as a victim. If you don't live all-out as a victor, life will take over, and you will end up just trying to survive. You will eventually have to deal with the grief (or the grief will deal with you).

Write your decision to live in victory in your journal. I have an example I like to use when I am making a positive change for my future. Think of the classic Christmas story, "A Christmas Carol" and the three ghosts: past, present, and future. Write this out in as much detail as you can. The more you connect to this exercise the more you enable your mind to change and heal.

FIRST: Journal your past.

- What do you want to learn from your past?
- What did you love about your past that you want to keep? (The reality is you cannot bring your loved one back but memories, behaviors, attitudes etc. can be kept.)
- What mistakes did you make in the past?
- What did those mistakes cost you?

- Power comes from being able to recognize mistakes and change them.

SECOND: Write what you presently need to change from your past to move forward. If you need to forgive yourself for those mistakes, then take the time and forgive yourself. But it is time to move forward in a positive direction.

- Where are you right now?
- Have you been living like a victim?
- Have you stuffed all your pain and just thrown yourself into work or worse—the internet?

- Write down a realistic picture of where you are right now emotionally, physically, etc.
- Write what you can do, adjust, or change right now to start living in victory.
- Decide, and write as many reasons why you must live in victory as you can think of.
- Write down what your life will look like if you do not make any changes; if you don't decide to live in victory.
- What would that life look like? Write down a clear picture of each choice.
- What are you missing out on right now?
- What could you be doing right now that you are not? It's important to see both sides and know that not only do you have a choice, you must make it. Tomorrow will come and the question is, will you have moved forward?
- Are there areas where you feel stuck? That's alright, just identify where you know you need to grow, heal,

or change. Write down each area along with possible solutions. If you need help with this, ask your grief counselor or grief coach.

THIRD: Write what your future life will look like because you choose victory today.

Write what it would look like if you decided it was just too much work, and you didn't choose victory. Don't be afraid to really tap into your emotions, the more real you are with yourself, the more likely you will change for the positive. This is a chance for you to dream.

- What have you always wanted to do?
- Where have you always wanted to go? This is your second chance to live your life all out! Allow this future to become real to you. On days when grief seems overwhelming, look at your journal and the future you desire.

Start the healing process now. There are serious consequences to stuffing your emotions away inside. Your health will suffer, you will probably look and feel ten years older, and your mental capacity will probably not be as sharp.

According to Don Colbert, M.D., "...Studies are linking more and more modern diseases to an epidemic of deadly emotions in our culture. Heart disease, hypertension, strokes, incidences of cancer, ulcers, skin diseases, and headaches all seem to be on the rise..."[1] Colbert also said, "The mind and body are linked. How you feel emotionally can determine how you feel physically. Certain emotions release hormones into the physical body that, in turn, can trigger the development of a host of diseases.

"Researchers have directly and scientifically linked emotions to hypertension, cardiovascular disease, and diseases related to the immune system. Studies have also highly correlated emotions with infections, allergies, autoimmune diseases, and headaches as well as other diseases."[2]

Even if you are reading this book a few years since your shattering, it is not too late to decide to be a victor over emotional stress.

Speak life and positive words over yourself. Use notecards. I know they seem old fashioned, but trust me, you will find them to be a powerful tool. When you are having a difficult time thinking of something positive to speak or think about, you can refer to a notecard. They are a perfect size to place under your visor in your vehicle, in a pocket or purse. Write positive sayings and quotes on each notecard. I even added some positive scriptures from the Bible so I could be armed with positive thoughts. When any condemning or negative thought comes to mind, pull out a notecard and read it out loud. Something I like to tell myself is that I have been created with purpose and have a great destiny to fulfill. You do also.

Author Napoleon Hill wrote, "Truly, thoughts are things, and powerful things at that, when they are mixed with definiteness of purpose, persistence..."[3] He understood the power of thoughts. Many things jump into our conscious mind, and you have the ability to decide which of those thoughts you will hang onto and believe.

English poet, William Ernest Henley wrote, "I am the master of my fate, I am the captain of my soul,"[4] The book of Proverbs found in the Bible was written by King Solomon of Israel, the wisest and richest man to ever live on earth. It is filled with wisdom. It was even taught in early American schools. Proverbs 23:7 says, "As he [she]] thinks in his [her] heart, so is he [she]…" The mistakes you might have made do not make you. Regardless of your religious beliefs, I recommend you read the book of Proverbs.

Big decisions like construction and remodeling need advice and oversight. In my case, I had to have my bathroom and closet remodeled. The construction worker I blindly trusted ended up leaving the company to start his own business after two months of partial work at my house. (Remember I was told the entire job would take four to five weeks.) I felt taken advantage of and betrayed all over again. The construction company ended up taking five months.

If any construction is necessary, get the advice and counsel of three people with knowledge of the construction field. Have at least one of those people review any contract before you sign. Get everything in writing such as: an approximate end date and expected cost. I hope sharing my very costly mistakes helps you avoid them.

chapter five

FROM HAMMERING TO HEALING

A DIVINE ENCOUNTER

Worn out from hammering that evidence bag, I was finally able to take a short, relaxing nap and head back to the conference. I sat in the back of the room hoping not to be noticed. The speaker, who had been friends with my husband, noticed me and asked me to come up to the front. A few of the speakers joined me there. They knew my mind and soul had been traumatized and wanted to pray over me.

What happened next, I can only describe as supernatural. Honestly, had I heard this story from someone else a year prior, I would have thought they were a bit crazy. What I have come to understand is that there are universal laws, for example (keeping things extremely simple and unscientific), The Law of Gravity discovered by Sir Isaac Newton around 1666 was not some new concept that Sir Newton developed. He simply put into words (and mathematical formulas) what already existed from the beginning of time.

A caveman that stepped off a steep cliff would fall until something like the ground stopped his fall. This would happen even if it occurred before the 'Law of Gravity' was discovered. The caveman did not have to believe in 'the Law of Gravity.' The principal remained the same whether he believed it or not. He stepped off the cliff and, therefore, he fell. Hopefully, we can agree on this very basic dumbed-down example

What I believe started at this conference was God simply revealing some universal laws of healing to me while He healed me. I do not believe I am more special than anyone else. I just think He knew I would want to share the experience with as many people as possible. I am saying all this just to say you do not have to believe in God in the same way I do in order to experience real and lasting healing. So, here is where it started.

I slowly walked to the front of the conference as the leaders met me. I felt my body become very heavy, so I sat down. The weight still seemed too much to bear so, I laid down on my back trying desperately to keep my eyes open because I thought someone might step on me.

My eyes shut so firmly nothing could have pried them open. I could feel my eyes starting to move back and forth under my eyelids. I could no longer hear the noise of the conference. It was like my spirit left my body and instantly was in a heavenly place. I don't know how to phrase this, but here's my best go of it. When my spirit was in that heavenly place, I had an understanding or 'knowing' of where I was and what was going on around me.

A spiritual being that was at least forty feet tall came over to me and showed me a large feather and then went away from me toward a boiling pot. It looked like something used to melt and purify gold. The spiritual being dipped the feather into what looked like liquid molten gold yet the feather didn't catch on fire or burn up. I could see the gold dripping off the feather as the angel approached me. I was still lying on the floor completely unable to move.

The being brushed the feather back and forth over both of my eyes as the hot liquid gold hit my eyes and then dripped to the floor. I could feel my eyes moving rapidly back and forth. I heard a voice saying, "I am burning away the images you saw of your husband when you found him after he shot himself in the face."

This occurred three times. On the third trip to burn my eyes, I also heard, "I am giving you a new image of Mike." The horrific image that was trapped in my mind terrifying me every time I tried to close my eyes was gone. I knew that seeing that image was gone. What a miracle! But what was my new image of Mike?

(There is a therapy that does something very similar, so if you have not experienced this type of miracle, no worries. It is called EMDR therapy, which stands for, 'Eye Movement Desensitization and Reprocessing' therapy.)

A NEW IMAGE

I could feel tears pouring out of my eyes as I had a moment of realizing my body was still laying on the floor at the conference. Then, immediately my spirit was back in the heavenly place. I could see hundreds of golden, almost amber colored stairs.

My heart filled with indescribable peace and joy. I saw what I perceived to be Jesus sitting about halfway up the stairs and Mike sitting one step below Him. He had his left arm around Mike and

Mike's head was resting on His chest directly over His heart. God was holding Mike like a parent would hold and comfort their child.

> I did not see Mike how I found him on
> February 12th, I saw his whole face.

Mike looked more handsome than ever. His face seemed to shine. Mike, my love, was at peace. All the questions I had wanted to ask Mike were completely gone at that moment. I could not think; I could not open my mouth. I could barely stand as I gazed on in complete silence. Peace continued to overwhelm every ounce of my being. I wanted desperately to stay right where I was for as long as I could. But …

In my spirit, I heard, "This is your new image of Mike, sitting with Me in complete peace. The trauma you saw has been burned away. When that horrible image tries to return, you must replace it with this new image."

What a crazy experience, yet it felt more real to me than anything. The question I had been begging to have answered: was Mike at peace? Now, I knew without one doubt that he was. More importantly, a supernatural Rapid Eye Movement Desensitization had been performed on me. I had been taught that when the traumatic image is removed (or desensitized), I needed to replace that image with a positive healthy image that brought peace.

It was more than a year later when I discovered 'Eye Movement Desensitization and Reprocessing' [EMDR] existed as a therapy. I did

EMDR therapy to heal from the last memory I had of Mike our home when he was drunk and frightening.

After Mike's death when I would look at where he had been sitting, a fear would come over me. EMDR therapy completely took away this fear. In the 'What Helped' section of this chapter I define EMDR therapy in more detail and how to find a professional in your area that uses it. I found it extremely beneficial. I would recommend EMDR therapy to anyone that has seen violence or tragedy. I can now look at the last place I saw Mike alive and feel a sense of peace.

WHAT HELPED

Consider Eye Movement Desensitization and Reprocessing therapy [EMDR]. EMDR therapy helps lessen the traumatic impact of witnessing or seeing tragedy or the aftermath. For more information, visit www.emdria.org. There you will find great information about EMDR Therapy for Children and Adolescents which can also be used on adults. If you are in the Kansas City area, www.EMDRGKC.com.

Pay attention to and filter your thoughts. Whether or not you recognize the thought as yours or not, if it isn't healthy, quit giving it space in your head. One of the thoughts I had (repeatedly) was, "You [Shawna] should have been completely aware of the family finances". Sure, I should have been not only aware of my family's finances, but I should have been helping with them. It was true. The question isn't whether it's 'true', but rather, is it healthy for me to continue to think about? The answer is NO.

This thought was about the past, something I cannot change. I can only start from today and move forward. This practice of releasing negative thoughts can also be referred to as "taking a thought captive". How do I do this? I say OUT LOUD, "I reject the lie that 'I'm a failure, I'm stupid...etc.' because I did not know my family's financial situation!"

(Something I need to interject right here is that with every condemning thought you have, there are negative emotions attached. So, in this example I felt like I was: stupid, a failure, incapable, lazy, a bad steward of my family's finances, and pretty much a complete loser. Are any of those feelings healthy? No. Maybe they could all be said about me truthfully, but this is about healing, not focusing on past mistakes. So, you may find yourself arguing in your head 'But it's true!' STOP! Forgive yourself and do this exercise.)

Ok, you have taken the thought and the accompanying negative emotions captive, now it is time to speak truth over yourself. Positive truth, said out loud. In my earlier example, I would say, "I now have the ability to learn how to take care of all my family's finances, and I have wisdom to budget".

The first time a negative thought comes into my head, I repent (which is saying I am sorry and turning away from the mistake I made of allowing it space in my mind). The negative thought might return, but I continue to reject and replace it with positive and healing truth.

Keep "pulling the weeds". As you regularly examine your thoughts, your mind will become much more peaceful. Yes, that means you will start to experience some real peace. I want to warn you that some of these thoughts are like a weed with a deep root. It may take pulling it out a few times before you finally remove the whole root. Be patient with yourself and the process. Add new, healthy thoughts that bring peaceful or joyful emotions each time you pull out the negative thought (weed).

You are in control and decide what you allow to stay in your head. The longer you have allowed a thought to stay, the more likely it has turned into a belief you now hold about yourself, others, God, or the world. If you have an unhealthy belief about yourself (which most people on the planet have) you can choose to break off that belief. It can be done in the same way you break off a negative thought. It sometimes takes more time, reinforcement of the healthy truth, and not allowing that belief to be spoken over you. Words are not simply hot air being blown out of us. Words have power. Even other people's words that are spoken over us have power, so please be careful who you allow to speak into your life.

One example includes words that we used while raising our children. We told them to never call someone 'stupid', or in any way imply the person was not smart. This was one of Mike's personal triggers. I learned this the hard way when we were dating. When I said that something he mentioned was 'ludicrous', Mike became enraged. I had no idea why, and at that time, I'm not sure if he knew why.

After we were married, he shared with me that while he was being beaten as a little boy, he was told he was stupid and would never amount to anything. Just telling me the story made him cry as all that pain resurfaced. This repetitive message formed into a belief he held about himself. The truth was that Mike was very intelligent. He was the first in his family to attend and graduate from university. Yet, even in his forties, Mike struggled with feeling he was not enough. Not 'good enough', or 'smart enough'. How powerful our words can be.

Maybe it was a long time ago when somebody whispered (or yelled) things over you that are not true. During a life-shattering tragedy, these thoughts often come back to haunt us. Take courage and the time to heal these old word-wounds, regardless of how long it has been. You can choose healthy, empowering new beliefs today.

Watch what you allow your eyes to see. If you witnessed a tragedy, then it is very important you do not allow more shattering images into your eyes/mind. Movies, TV shows, video games or even people may trigger unhealthy thoughts or visions. You never know when one of these things might pop up so it is important to be vigilant. One of the ways you can prepare is by having positive quotes/thoughts written down (like on a notecard) and ready to look at if you have to take a thought or image captive.

You are doing great things to heal. I know it takes time to do these steps, but time will pass whether you do them or not. You are learning tools that can bring healing and joy back into your life. You are also learning how to let that joy shine through every crack as pieces of your life are put back together. I promise you that once you start using these tools, your life can become even more beautiful than it was before you were shattered.

chapter six

THE IMPORTANCE OF A TRIBE

FINDING OUR COUNSELOR

My toenail polish was finally starting to fade. I had gotten a pedicure before Mike and went to Cancun in January. I refused to take the toenail polish off because I felt as long as it was there, Mike was somehow still with me. It had been over a month and a half since Mike died and almost all of my toenail polish was gone. As I looked at my toes, and pondered how quickly the time had passed, I realized the importance of starting grief counseling for me and my kids as soon as possible. My experience is, the sooner you begin (especially if you are responsible for children), the easier the healing process will be for both you and your children.

A woman I knew who had retired from counseling offered her services to the three of us for absolutely no charge. She was an excellent counselor and I felt blessed that she was able and willing to work with us. Michael wanted to see a male counselor, but agreed to see my friend until he was able to get through a waiting list for a male counselor.

By the time Celeste and I started with our counselor, I had received Mike's death certificate and Celeste was asking other people how her daddy had taken his life. I talked with our counselor about the best way to tell her. I already told Celeste that her daddy had taken his own life but never told her any details. We decided I would allow Celeste to read the death certificate in a counselling session and I would stand nearby if she had any questions or wanted to say anything.

I wanted to protect her from the horrible truth of her daddy's suicide but knew if I didn't tell her, someone else would and who knows what they might say incorrectly. Celeste had not cried much since first hearing about her daddy's death. I think she was in shock and disbelief. I watched from about a hundred feet away while Celeste read the detailed and way-too-specific death certificate. Our counselor stood beside her for what felt like hours. A few minutes later, Celeste finally walked over to me and I just held her as we cried. Please, be the one to tell your children what happened using age appropriate language.

I found out while I was writing this chapter that Celeste was told by a family member that she needed to be strong for her family! This made her worry even more about Michael and me. That was a very unhealthy thing to tell a twelve-year-old whose daddy just took his life.

Jordan was told everything, all at once, by his mom the night I called. That was a lot of information for an eighteen-year-old to hear about the man he looked up to and admired. Jordan shared about his dad with a few of his friends in England who had never met his dad. Someone told Jordan what a selfish thing his dad had done.

> When you are hurting, the last thing you want or need to hear are negative statements about the person you just lost.

People seem compelled to share their scary and disturbing suicide stories with someone who has just experienced something similar. I wish I could tell you that those who care about you will always say the right things, but we both know better. I suggest that you initially give them grace. People want to make us feel better but have no idea how. It's human nature to want to relate. Unfortunately, this is the last thing we need or want.

I do recommend interrupting anyone sharing their 'suicide story' as quickly as you can. I give some specific suggestions on what to say or how you might handle these situations in the 'What Helped' section after this chapter. Many of our friends did not know how to treat me or my children which meant their comments were more hurtful than helpful.

SIDE EFFECTS OF STRESS

During this time, I cried so hard that I actually burst a vein from my right eye to my hairline. Still in shock, I had not gotten more than three hours of sleep in one night since the night before I found Mike. I would go into my closet every night around 3 or 4 a.m.

and I would cry and pray out loud. On March 22, 2014, I wrote this note to God:

> *"I've been praying and worshiping you in my closet for the last forty-five minutes. You say in the Bible that, 'You are a father to the fatherless and a defender of the widows."* (Psalms 68:5 WEB) *"I'm asking You, God, to be my kids' daddy. I need You to show up in a real way. We need to feel your hugs, and your love. Please, please come to us."*

I knew that it would be too much for my kids to see me completely fall apart, but I learned from my counselor that it was alright to let them see me cry. When Michael was only eight years old, he told me that he didn't want to cry because he didn't want to upset me. I needed to learn how to balance crying with being strong for them. I also needed to listen when they were upset and needed to cry, instead of always joining in their crying.

Sometimes, while the children were in school, I just held my Bible to my chest and cried. I had not been able to read it because my eyes were always filled with tears. My back hurt so much that it was difficult to straighten up. I would have to lay flat on the floor and breathe just so I could walk again. Yet another great side effect of stress: I would hyperventilate or have a panic attack at least a couple times a week. During one of those attacks, my mother and my sister just laid on top of me, held me, and told me how much they loved me.

Shortly after that experience, I went to see my counselor. I was feeling that gut-wrenching pain as every fiber inside me cried. I felt so empty in my weeping. She sat beside me and hugged me. Then through my tears I cried out:

"Where are you, God? Why can't I feel you? I desperately need to feel you, God, and I don't feel you. I need your love! I need you to hug me,"

I even quoted verses from my Bible that said God was my comforter. (See Jeremiah 8:18 NIV) I yelled out, "Why can't I feel the God I read about in the Bible?" My deep hurt turned to utter frustration.

IDENTIFYING MY TRIBE

Three or four years prior to this session, my daughter's Girl Scout troop went to the Omaha Zoo in Nebraska. All the Girl Scouts and their families got to spend the night in the aquarium at the zoo. When the zoo closed, we all got a private tour. It was amazing to see all the animals and the zoo after hours.

When we got to the lion's area, two of the female lions were messing with each other. A male lion closely watched their interaction. The male lion let out a little growl as if to say, enough is enough. It was a great show. We all started walking to the next exhibit when the female lions started to fight. The male lion got up on all fours and let out a powerful roar! I had never heard anything like that before.

Everyone in our group literally jumped back as the roar vibrated through the whole zoo. It felt like my bones were shaking. I finally understood why the male lion was called 'The King of the Jungle'.

While I was in this specific counselling session, crying out in frustration for God, I heard a voice more terrifying than that of the lion. I looked up to see who had walked into the room, but there was no one. Then I heard the voice again. I believe the audible voice I was hearing was God's. This voice was not a sweet, soft, comforting voice like what I imagined would come from Him.

The voice was full of power and awe. Every part of my body was shaking, even my mouth. My counselor was still holding me.

"Did you hear that?" I asked my counselor.

"No," she said.

I still believed everything I believed from the Bible prior to Mike taking his own life, but now however, I was crying out for actual proof. I never dared question God, but in my brokenness, I cried out for God in a new way. I expected what I had read in the Bible to be real, and if it was real, then I should be able to experience what it said was for me!

He said, *"I am here! I am holding you! The very breath you are taking is Me. I am breathing for you through your pastors."*

I pictured memories of myself lying on the floor trying to catch my breath, hyperventilating and wondering where my next dollar would come from. My mind flooded with memories of my pastors helping financially and gathering others to help pay my bills. I saw myself taking deep cleansing breaths as each bill was miraculously paid. Wow, God was breathing for me through my pastors.

Next, I heard God say, *"My arms are wrapped around you. I am holding you. I am holding you through your sister and parents."*

Another picture flashed in front of me of when they were laying on top of me holding me with their arms tightly wrapped around me.

Then I heard, *"You can feel Me holding you. I am holding you up. I am walking for you through your friends and church family."*

HIS HANDS AND FEET

This experience felt like six hours, yet I think it was only minutes. My body was still shaking and I could not speak. I was keenly aware of my 'smallness' compared to the voice I had just heard. As I sat in counseling still unable to speak or move, I remembered many things my tribe had done and were still doing for me.

We are designed to live in community, to be others' hands and feet, showing love to each other in tangible ways. I experienced this firsthand. My tribe was walking for me when I could no longer walk. They were carrying me when I could not go on.

For example, one of my friends set up a website posting things our family needed from tissues and fuzzy socks to basic food. She spent hours helping me sign up for Social Security, and getting the kids on insurance. I could not have walked through this without her and people like her. Friends even came over to clean my house. They did whatever was needed. Sometimes they just sat with me. This was my tribe in action, and God was present in my life through them.

My tears finally stopped and I was able to leave counseling. I don't remember saying a word, as it all seemed so surreal. I held every word God said close to my heart. I wrote everything down that I heard that day, but I was unable to speak about this experience for months.

> It was truly breathtaking to see that God cared about every detail of my life down to tissues to blow my nose.

I AM HERE

Over the next few weeks, I noticed other ways God showed up through my tribe. Here are some examples:

- At my next counselling session, my counselor suggested adding a 'hugger' to the end of our time. This was so therapeutic. The 'hugger' was a woman from my church who seemed to spill love every time she hugged someone. My 'hugger' faithfully attended the last fifteen minutes of my counseling sessions. She would lovingly and safely hug me as I learned new ways to heal.

- One day, I was feeling especially lonely because everybody I knew was married, but I didn't know where I fit anymore. So, I decided to drive Mike's car to his cemetery gravesite. The gravesite was muddy from the melting snow and no grass was growing but I was in too much pain to care. I laid face down in the mud, crying out to God about how lonely I felt. Next thing I knew, an SUV came driving down the little cemetery road and I was frustrated that I would have to get up from my pity party to move Mike's car.

As the vehicle got closer, I saw my dear friend. She told me she had a strange urge to go to Starbucks in the middle of the day. From the store, she could see Mike's parked car, so she immediately drove over. She was horrified to find me lying face down in the mud crying. She sat beside me and cried with me. Soon the two of us were laughing and sharing funny stories of Mike. I remembered the first thing I heard God say to me, "I AM HERE!" God was truly there through my friend who showed up when I needed company, love, and comfort.

I absolutely knew God was with me. I could not hide from Him, even in the mud. Many of the people who helped me were old friends I had isolated myself from when Mike and I were having ups and downs in our marriage. Maybe you can relate? Yet, here they were, back in my life as if we never missed a beat. What an amazing blessing! Before Mike died, I really didn't feel like I had many friends. Between working, raising our children, and volunteer counseling I did not have much time. I learned how important true friends are.

WHAT HELPED

Find a support group for those who have also lost someone. Once you have already begun grief counseling on your own and are ready, a helpful step is to locate and physically go to a grief support group. (I found that I needed individual counseling first before I could sit in a group.) Many churches have support groups focusing on older widows and widowers, so just find out in advance if it will be a place you feel comfortable. Solace House is a center for grieving and healing. It is a program of Kansas City Hospice and Palliative Care. I put their information in the back of this book. Many cities have similar programs and some hospitals and community centers also offer support groups.

If you don't have anything like this near your home, I offer virtual coaching and virtual support groups online because I know how important both of these elements are to the healing process. For more information, visit www.shawnamertel.com or email Shawnamertel@gmail.com.

Allow the right people to help you. Family can sometimes be the worst help. Often, they are also grieving. Have the courage to be around and ask for help from the healthier people you know. Let them support you in the tasks that seem impossible or overwhelming. There will also likely be people who emerge from your outer circle and become instrumental in your healing.

Let those in your tribe know it is okay to talk about and say the name of your lost loved one. Often others will not bring up the person, especially by name, because they think it might be upsetting. I asked someone who I knew loved Mike very much why they never talked about him. They said because they didn't want to remind me or my kids. Sounds pretty ridiculous as you read it, but believe it or not, many people think that if they just don't mention our loss, we'll forget all about them.

We will never forget them. However, as we continue the work of grieving, we will be able to remember the great things they brought to our lives and how lucky we were to share life with them even if only for a short while

Crying is good and it heals. I used to think of crying as a weakness and would not let my kids see me cry. I'm not saying you should fall apart and cry continually around your children or family. I'm just saying it is an act of courage to be humble enough to allow others to see you cry. Washington Irving said, "There is sacredness in tears. They are not the mark of weakness, but of power. They speak more eloquently than ten thousand tongues. They are the messengers of overwhelming grief…unspeakable love."[1]

Over time, as you continue to take steps forward, the pain will decrease but the love will not, and joy will indeed return.

chapter seven

BRAVE STEPS IN THE AFTERMATH

VISITING THE GRAVESITE

Weeks after Mike's death, I decided to take my children to the gravesite. I wish I had been a little more prepared. My daughter bought a glass plaque to place on her daddy's gravesite. It read:

> "Dad, if you've ever wondered if you are appreciated, YOU ARE AND ALWAYS WILL BE, more than words can ever say."

As Celeste sweetly placed the plaque on the cross, I read the words on it for the first time. I couldn't help but cry. Michael cried also until he finally asked to return to the van. That was the only time I 'made' them go to the gravesite with me.

We all grieve so differently, and I'm much more prepared when we visit the site now. In Chapter 8's What Helped section, I discuss things you can do at the gravesite yourself or with your children. If your loved one was cremated, there are suggestions for that as well.

I knew Mike's spirit was in heaven yet his body was right there below the ground. I loved his spirit but I also loved his body. It hurt when some well-meaning person would tell me that my husband wasn't really in the cemetery. You have probably heard all kinds of hurtful, terrible, or even sometimes shocking things as well. We all could probably write a book on what NOT to say to somebody whose world has been shattered.

I encourage you to forgive them and release that hurt. You have enough healing to do. It might help to get a journal and label it 'things not to say'. If you are reading this as someone wanting to know how to help, you have an amazing gift of empathy. Thank you for wanting to learn more on how to best use your good intentions. Unless such a loss actually happens to you, books like this will be the best source of what to say, what not to say, or when to just stand beside the family and say nothing at all.

CHANGING ROLES

I felt like I was entering the 'twilight zone'. Since Mike's death, everything in my life had come to a screeching halt and time seemed strangely slow. I counted each day of the month, dreading every twelfth because it was the monthly anniversary of Mike's death. Since my experience with the angel in Heaven, I was sleeping three to five hours a night. This was a huge improvement, but not enough to help me cover all aspects of parenting.

When Mike was alive, we shared many of the parenting roles. Now, I was trying to be both mom and dad for my children which did not work well for me. I suggest not trying to be both parents. When a loved one dies, our roles in life often change. We learn many new things (some we never planned on learning) as our parenting responsibility expands.

> I learned the hard way that regardless of how much I tried, I could never fill the role of daddy.

I strongly encourage you to accept that you cannot fill the role of your lost loved one either. You will probably be taking on many new roles and learning many new things, as I did. In the What Helped section after this chapter, I give some suggestions on better ways of handling these new roles. I ended up with several bloody lips from wrestling and almost broke my back trying to carry Michael Jr. upstairs to bed if he fell asleep in the van.

One of the many new roles I had to learn was how to plan an out of town trip. There was a conference being held in Moravian Falls, North Carolina. I knew it would be very healing and it was important for me to attend. Celeste also wanted to go, and I knew it would benefit her as well. I was nervous because it had been over fifteen years since I planned a trip without help. Not having a credit card also made traveling extremely difficult.

There was an additional reason I wanted to attend. Mike's only brother was volunteering at the conference. He lived close by and was able to pick us up from the airport. It was comforting to visit with him especially because he reminded me of Mike in so many positive ways.

Later that night when we finally arrived at the hotel, the clerk looked at me sadly and told me my card had been declined. *Declined? How could that be?* I used this debit card to secure my room. I thought I did everything correctly. I made sure enough cash was in my account to cover the room, meals, everything. I had even told the bank I was traveling to North Carolina. The bank neglected to tell me that the debit card could only be used in a handful of states outside Missouri. You can probably guess by now what I did next...cried and cried! After about ten to fifteen minutes, I pulled myself together. The hotel clerk allowed me to pay cash for the first night and I trusted that I would work something out with my bank the next day.

So many thoughts and emotions suddenly filled my mind as I walked around and saw people who knew Mike. It was so difficult, I felt like I was reliving the funeral.

- Mike had been to Moravian Falls many times to volunteer, but I had only been once.
- Many people at the conference knew Mike and just found out he had taken his own life.
- Others knew but were not able to attend the funeral.
- Everyone that knew Mike loved him and now they were all flooding me with hugs, tears, and, of course, questions.

BRIGHTON'S VISION

Brighton was a young boy who knew Mike from various conferences they attended in other states. When his parents saw me at a conference, they told him Mike had passed away a few weeks prior. Brighton had had a vision of Mike that he wanted me to know about. Brighton told me he was sitting in heaven on some golden steps beside Mike.

Brighton told me Mike was happy and that he had asked Mike, "Why?" Mike said, "Because I get to drive my favorite car, my dream car." That didn't sound very "holy"! Of course, I wanted to hear things like, how much Mike loved me and the kids, how sorry he was that he took his life—anything like that. But, in his ten-year-old voice, Brighton continued describing everything he saw and heard.

Brighton said Mike had a pair of keys on a keyring. Mike was twirling the keyring around on his middle finger. My stomach sank as I remembered many times I had seen Mike put his keyring on his middle finger and spin his keys around. Then Brighton really took my breath away when he said, "And this is how Mike was sitting", and Brighton leaned back exactly how Mike would do when he was happy and excited and maybe up to something silly.

There's no way Brighton could have known this or have imitated Mike with such precision. Also, Mike didn't even drive when he would travel to Moravian Falls. I had no doubt Brighton was telling me the truth, plus there was no reason for him to lie.

TELL ME MORE ABOUT THE CAR, BRIGHTON

Mike never told anyone about his dream car except for me. I asked Mike one time why he didn't want the kids to know. He shared it was because he wanted his kids to think that he was already driving his dream car. That's exactly how Mike was; he didn't want the kids or me to think he was sacrificing what he wanted to give to us. Mike was a huge giver in so many ways.

I asked Brighton to describe exactly what kind of car he saw. Brighton said, "It's a yellow sports car. The name was 'Co' or maybe Corvette?" He wasn't sure because he had never seen this type of sports car before. He could only say he was sure the name started with a C. Uncle Steve asked if it could be a Camaro. Someone pulled up a picture on their smart phone. Uncle Steve thought of a Camaro because their dad had an old Camaro and it had always been their dad's dream to fix it up.

When Brighton saw the picture on the phone, he was seeing Mike's dream car. Brighton went on to say the car was bright yellow with two black racing stripes. When I had watched the movie Transformers with Mike, Bumblebee had transformed into the new yellow Camaro. Mike had told me that was his all-time dream car. Mike even wanted it yellow with the two black stripes. I asked Brighton if he had ever seen the movie Transformers. He said he had not.

Brighton described Mike's dream car exactly. I knew, absolutely knew without one doubt that this little boy had not only been to heaven but he had sat beside and talked with Mike. I was the only one that would recognize the silly expressions Mike would make when he was holding back extreme joy and Brighton had mimicked him precisely.

My idea of what people do in heaven was completely wrong. I thought there would only be a bunch of angels and people holding candles, floating around and singing. I had no idea you could drive your dream car! I know this sounds crazy, but why limit God? God's love isn't controlled by our idea of who He's going to talk to or who He's going to show heaven to. God seems to use the most unlikely, the young, like Brighton, or the hot mess like me to display His love.

> I'm thankful he shared his vision with me and didn't change it up to make it sound more 'holy' or what I wanted to hear.

I'm glad I pushed through and finished the conference trip. It gave me confidence as I embarked on the next adventure. Had I crumbled and left at the first sign of distress, I would have missed out on that priceless exchange with Brighton.

BE PROUD OF YOURSELF

Each new thing you try or learn needs to be documented in a journal. I know that sounds kind of silly, especially since you should already be keeping a journal about how you are feeling and what you are doing to deal with those feelings. This new journal will help you on days you are feeling overwhelmed or pushed beyond your limits. Now, you can look at it and be proud of yourself for all the new roles or new task you have started doing.

I started taking care of all the bills and budget. I am and have been learning many things about computers. I shifted from the fun parent to the parent. I still love to have fun with my kids, but now I discipline, plan family activities, help with all homework, do bedtime routines, and supervise morning routines. You get the picture.

We take on certain roles based on our personalities and strong suits and perhaps your roles have changed drastically as mine did. Don't be embarrassed when you come across something you don't know how to do even if it appears the rest of the world (including your kids) can do it. For example, my daughter has helped me out on the computer, and I took a class about finance and budgeting. We are still a work in progress.

LAWYERS, LIARS AND PROBATE COURT

There were giant obstacles I had to face in the aftermath of Mike's death. Things like: he had no will, huge amounts of debt I was not aware of, my name was not on anything (especially the house), and I had no credit. Two life insurance policies refused to pay out.

I had to acknowledge my willful ignorance of our financial situation and forgive myself for not being wise with our money, and for not being a better partner to Mike by helping him manage it all. I also felt like I needed to look to God in this probate situation. Three different expert lawyers who helped prepare the probate case told me that my probate would take at least a year or more because of all the obstacles.

Even though these intelligent, well-meaning experts had their informed opinions, they were wrong. If your situation seems hopeless or bleak, never lose hope. I wrote in my journal, "Thank you, God, for supplying all of my needs." I felt like God gave me a specific date that all of this would be handled and I wrote the date down.

On May 20, 2014, a judge from the Jackson County Circuit Court ordered: "No letters shall be issued on or against said estate." The court ordered that all creditors or other interested parties attempting to collect from my husband be stopped. The probate case was over on the exact date I had written down. Mike died on February 12, 2014, so by this point barely three months had passed, and I'm still not sure when probate had actually been filed.

The creditors and interested parties had wanted to take my home and belongings so they could be sold for repayment. With one stroke of the gavel, the judge gave me a six-figure reversal of debt! A true miracle. I could write a whole book on each amazing financial miracle. What earthly wisdom said would take at least nine months to eighteen months, was over in less than three months.

FACING THE STORM

I was once told a story about how ships survive large storms in the vast ocean. It fascinated me because it seemed opposite of what I would choose to do to survive. The ship must turn and face directly into the storm. If the ship tries to turn away from a large wave, it will capsize or turn over. We must do the same. We must face our problems head-on. Running away from or ignoring a bad situation doesn't solve anything and usually makes things worse. Using anything to numb our pain just delays a solution and creates additional problems.

WHAT HELPED

Stop judging yourself. Those in our situation are quick to believe advice from someone who has never been in our shoes. They can't know what we should be feeling. There is no time table for grief. Don't box yourself in.

Get rid of your limiting beliefs. Don't allow others (even experts) to define what is possible in the aftermath of tragedy.

Write out meaningful quotes, scriptures, and affirmations dealing with the specific need or concern you have. Write three to four of these out on notecards and keep them with you. Read them out loud throughout your day and ask for wisdom on how to handle a particular problem.

Take one brave step at a time. It would be rare for you to only have one specific need or problem after a life-shattering tragedy but there are strategies and priorities to handle first. Taking steps toward healing the enormous pain of grief you are experiencing is vital. As you heal, start addressing other urgent situations. Focus on one problem at a time. You can completely immobilize yourself if you try to take on too much at one time.

- **Write down the problems you are facing on separate sheets of paper while in a safe place, like counseling.** Label each problem with (a) Now. (b) In a week or two, (c) Can wait a couple months (d) Can wait 6 months +. Put pages (c) and (d) in an easily marked folder and file it away. Look at your page marked '(a) Now' and ask yourself:

  - Who has knowledge to help me?
  - Who do I trust to help me?
  - Do I know how to handle this?
  - When can I handle this?

After you have asked and answered these questions, place the pages in the order they need to get handled. Now look at (b) In a week or two; and go through the same process. Make folders for each time period that you have determined each problem fits into. Put all the folders away except the first one, (a) Now.

You might have several issues that are pressing. Make sure the pressing issues are only yours and your family's. Others will approach you with many things that appear like they need immediate attention. Creditors will try to scare you into thinking they can destroy you. Don't be intimidated. If you have several 'Now' problems, go through the questions I gave you. Ask for help and work through one at a time.

People want to help you, they just feel helpless on how, so don't be afraid to ask. You might find out you have more friends than you thought. If somebody can completely solve one of your problems, let them, but set up a date of completion.

Live! I don't know how else to say it. You are still living in spite of whatever life-shattering tragedy that occurred. You are alive and you have a purpose. You know how fragile life can be so make every moment count. Every day you have with your loved ones is a gift. Remember those gifts, and cherish them.

Be willing to go places where you know you can experience healing. I'm not advising you to go into debt just to go somewhere or try to run away from your problems. However, if you have a place that makes you feel safe, happy, or at peace, I would recommend trying to go there for a weekend. Sometimes, when we are near where tragedy occurred, we find it difficult to think as clearly as when we get away. Use this time for healing.

Remember children's emotional and intellectual development affects their understanding. We can help them by providing honest, age-appropriate information and listening to their responses. See Appendix B.

Consistently reassure your children of your love for them and that you will not leave them. After Mike's death, both of my younger children needed constant reassurance that I loved them, and more importantly, I was not leaving them. I remember for months I would take an hour and a half just tucking Michael Jr. in bed and reading the Bible over him. Then I would go into my daughter's room and spend another hour with her.

When children lose a parent in such a tragic way, they need extra time with the remaining parent. Talk about funny things and good memories. Make sure your kids know it is okay and even good for them to talk and cry about the loved one they lost.

chapter eight

THE INVESTIGATION

After Mike died, I began 'my investigation'. Why would the man I loved so much, the one who loved me with all of his heart, take his own life? I know Mike loved his children more than mere words could express.

So, why?

Why?

WHY?

Why would he put an assault rifle under his chin and pull the trigger? Why would he leave us that way?

I had no immediate answers, but I had to find out why. I became like a detective somehow believing if I had known the reason why, I could have changed the outcome.

I discovered he had secretly been drinking for about two to three months. I found alcohol hidden throughout the house, garage and even outside. Our business had a great month in October 2013. In November, Mike got very sick. From what I've pieced together, he must have stopped working our business. I didn't notice because his routine of leaving the house every morning didn't change. Two weeks before he took his life, he told me about the debt on his mother's credit card and the argument they had had. I knew he could earn enough money to pay it off in a few weeks (especially when we worked together) so I hadn't been exceptionally alarmed.

> I wish he would have reached out to
> somebody, anybody, but he did not.

After a few months had passed, I was finally ready to attempt to work with the VA again. They denied even the measly $200.00 for his burial which was just cruel considering Mike served his country well as a Captain and left the service with an honorable discharge.

Here I was in a little satellite VA office and the employee pulled up Mike's file on the computer. While attempting to help me, he was called away by a superior and left the room. He happened to leave his computer screen on so, I looked over and started reading some of what Mike did in Somalia which included details of how he helped retrieve some of our murdered and mutilated American soldiers. After reading that, I quickly returned to my seat with much more understanding of why Mike refused to discuss Somalia.

This is where much of his PTSD (Post Traumatic Stress Disorder) came from. It is shocking to see a mutilated body, especially when it's someone you knew and cared about. I had been through it myself after finding Mike. I could not even imagine the pain Mike must have felt from what he experienced in Somalia. No wonder he refused to talk about it.

I got up and left the VA office. There was nothing they could do to help me financially or otherwise, but I did have a piece of the puzzle.

PTSD, RED TAPE AND NO FOLLOW-UP

Mike never received help for his PTSD, so he never had an official diagnosis. He stuffed it all deep inside and refused to even talk about it. Once, about six years before Mike took his life, I witnessed him experiencing a PTSD flashback. At the time, I had no idea what was going on with Mike, I just knew when I looked into his eyes, and he was not the same man I knew. His eyes were almost black where normally they were a beautiful blue. He was hurting me, something he would never even threaten to do and completely opposite of his personality. Suddenly, his eyes returned to blue, and he just looked at me, stunned.

Then he asked me, "What happened?"

He had no memory of the whole incident. Knowing now about what Mike experienced and saw in Somalia, I have no doubt he had PTSD. I believe if Mike had dealt with the trauma from his past, he would still be here today.

I strongly encourage you to deal with any and all trauma you have experienced. I know this has already been said, but it is so important. In the early 2000's, PTSD was not widely discussed, especially among the strong and brave personnel of our military or first responders. These days, even small towns have access to therapists that specialize in PTSD.

Mike attempted to get help from the VA hospital in the Kansas City area several years before, but never got a proper diagnosis or any treatment. The VA prescribed antidepressants, but could not see Mike for any follow up for over six weeks. By then, the medicine was gone. He never received a quality evaluation and never attempted another round of antidepressants again.

THE ROLE ALCOHOL PLAYED

When Mike would drink, those memories would resurface. Once he started, he couldn't stop himself until he passed out. The next three to four days after Mike drank too much, he would be filled with anger and rage. Our children never really saw this because I kept them away until the anger passed.

I started to suspect Mike had a drinking problem about two to three years into our marriage. It took that long because his frequency didn't appear to be what I thought an alcoholic's looked like. I thought alcoholics drank every day. Mike would go three to six months without drinking. Then he would drink until he passed out. He could not seem to stop. I learned this is also the behavior of an alcoholic.

Mike told me about his childhood and the difficulty of being raised by an alcoholic mom. I know he never completely healed from that trauma. I encouraged him to talk to his mother about it and tell her he forgave her. Mike had also not healed from the physical abuse he endured in his childhood. Anger and hurt remained deep in his soul. Certain words and phrases said to Mike during the abusive sessions of his youth were totally forbidden in our home. We never said, "Stupid" or anything related to being stupid. The phrases, "You will never amount to anything!" and "You are worthless!" still echoed in Mike's heart. He heard them internally every time he messed up.

In 2005, Mike had lost his job. Our side business was declining and I had been extremely ill for a year and a half. During this time, we were blessed with our son, Michael Jr. When Michael Jr. was about eighteen-months-old, Mike went on a two-day drinking binge. The two days that followed were filled with anger and he actually attacked me. I believe this was a PTSD flashback – a door opened by alcohol.

For the first time in our marriage, I was afraid of him. I knew he was not in his right mind when he hurt me, but I didn't know what was going on. I had never seen PTSD so up close and personal before. That was Mike's 'rock bottom' and the first time he realized he needed help. It scared us both.

Mike immediately sought counseling. We also started going to a different church, and he found accountability with our new pastor. Despite these great strides, what Mike did not do was deal with the trauma from verbal and physical abuse he suffered as a child. He also did not deal with or heal the trauma and PTSD from Somalia.

The other things Mike did for help actually helped. He would go nine to twelve months without drinking and then, without warning, fall off the wagon, get completely drunk, and be angry for a few days. Slowly, things would rebuild to "normal".

At the time, I didn't fully appreciate the deep wounds, pain, and trauma Mike had not allowed to surface and be healed. I knew how valuable that was because I had found freedom from my childhood sexual abuse and subsequent eating disorder. Once you heal from the past, it can no longer hold you captive. Your past can no longer whisper in your ear: "You are no good," or "You are what you have done in your past." You can be free from those accusations.

"TRUST ME WITH YOUR WHY"

I knew it was important for me and the children to see Mike's brother, Steve, and their cousin, Zach, so I drove Jordan, Celeste and Michael to Greensboro, North Carolina, almost a thousand miles away and two days of driving. We stayed with Uncle Steve in his apartment for a night. The following day, we all drove another two-hundred miles to Myrtle Beach to spend a week on vacation all together.

Every morning at Myrtle Beach, I would get up and go for a run alone to just meditate. I kept asking, "Why did Mike leave me? Why did he leave his children?" The asking would turn to begging as I pleaded to God for answers.

One day after running a good distance, I heard in my spirit, "Stop asking 'Why?'"

Surely God was not asking me to stop my investigation?

I said, "I have to know why Mike left me and the children! I know Mike loved us so WHY would he leave us?"

I heard it louder this time asking, "Do you love Me?"

I said, "Yes, God. You know how much I love you!"

Then I heard very clearly, "Do you love Me enough to give Me your 'why'?"

I ran at least one more mile pondering what I had just heard in my spirit. I think He wanted me to stop my investigation? Really?

One last time I heard, "Do you love me enough to give me your 'why'? Trust Me with your 'why.'"

My knees bent as I hit the sand, followed by a complete face plant. I wept. "I ask you, do you love yourself enough to lay down your 'why'? Do you love your children enough? Do you desire peace enough?"

> Somehow, I mistakenly believed that if I had all the answers and knew all the reasons why Mike took his life, I could bring him back.

The painful reality was soul-crushing. Nothing I did or found out could ever bring Mike back to me and our children. No 'why' would ever be enough.

"Give me your 'why,'" I heard.

As I laid in the sand crying, a gentle, loving voice whispered in my ear, "There will never be an answer that could ever satisfy you."

Finally, I said out loud, "God, I love You. I will stop investigating. I will stop asking 'why'. I put my trust in You."

I laid in the sand crying, telling God I needed His peace. The truth is there is never a good enough reason why someone takes their life. Deep down, you and I both already know that. That day on Myrtle Beach I surrendered my right to ask why. I felt like a piece of me was dying. What kept my mind occupied when the kids were sleeping or gone was over. Now, there was no puzzle to solve. To my surprise, there was a part of me that felt free. I was free to live without carrying the burden of why my husband took his own life.

I finally pulled myself up from the sand and began walking back to the hotel. My feet felt a little lighter and my shoulders lifted a little higher. Peace did start to replace my once unquenchable desire to know why Mike took his life.

I had coached so many people on how to heal so I "knew" these wounds, hurts and traumas needed to be healed—must be healed! Regardless of what circumstances occurred prior to Mike taking his life, there was nothing I or anyone could *do* or *know* on this side of it that would change anything. I also completely understood that Mike's choice was not my fault, my children's fault, his mother's fault, or anyone else's fault. We are all responsible for how we choose to live our life or take it. It wasn't even the military's fault. That is difficult to say because I desperately wanted to blame someone…anyone.

STARTING A NEW NORMAL

The rest of summer 2014 with Jordan flew by quickly. It came time for him to return to London and start University. Celeste was entering middle school as a seventh grader and Michael was going into third grade. I wanted to hold on to all three of them and not let them go.

Jordan made many new friends but most of them didn't know what had happened to his dad. Celeste was looking forward to a fresh start in middle school where only a handful of her peers knew what had happened to our family. Michael Jr., on the other hand, was at the same elementary school with the same children.

It seemed like everyone at his school knew. It was sad and difficult when parents would not allow their child to come into our home or worse, not allow their kids to play in our yard. It was also a blessing for Michael because he had become best friends with a boy that was amazing and a true friend. All his teachers were so supportive, and the principal even put Michael and his best friend in the same class. He was able to renew his confidence just knowing that his buddy had his back.

WHAT HELPED

Stop investigating and stop asking why! There will never be a good enough answer where you would say, "Oh that's why. Now it makes complete sense." It seems crazy even as I type it out. There is no WHY that can satisfy what you have been through!

By now you know the brutal truth—your loved one is gone and they are not coming back. I know if we could go back in time, we all would. Since that is not an option, we must go forward. I'm not at all suggesting you forget your loved one because it's not possible. Investigating and asking questions that have no good answers can't change what happened. They only keep you from healing.

It's time to have a funeral for your questions. Maybe you have a few people in your life that you feel safe enough to share your 'could haves',' would haves', or 'should haves' with.

Tell them upfront you DO NOT want answers and that you are officially ending the questioning. You are simply asking them to help or at least stand by you. Bury those questions, cremate them, just get rid of them! This tragedy was NOT your fault, so stop blaming yourself.

It is also time to stop asking questions that hold back your ability to heal and find joy again. After a funeral, wake, or ceremony, there is usually food or celebrating. Celebrate that you are now free from these limiting questions. The next person that rudely asks you "Why?" simply say, "I buried (cremated) that question, and I'm not willing to dig it up. Sorry."

If you follow their "why" with a question, there's an awkward pause while they figure out how insensitive it was that they asked. If you need a rescue script, here are some good redirection questions:

- Do you have any funny or happy memories of them you can share with me?
- How long did you know them?
- How did you meet?
- What did you enjoy doing with them?

Think of some healthy questions and write them in your journal. If you need to, put them on notecards (or in your cellphone). Don't get caught off guard or go blank. You might be surprised by the funny or happy things you learn. Write those things down, too.

It's too soon and you aren't over it yet. I was told by many that 'time would heal.' By now, you know it does NOT. Although I knew that, I subconsciously counted the days since Mike took his life. Plus, something that was NOT helpful was every 12th of the month (which was the date of Mike's death), I would mourn. It was like this morbid anniversary I couldn't get out of my mind. I wondered why nobody else seemed to acknowledge this day but me. Of course, most people didn't even know.

Some people were starting to think and unfortunately say things like, "Aren't you over that by now?" "Hasn't he been dead for about half a year?" "You should try dating..." By now, you might be receiving similar rude questions or comments, so I have two suggestions that helped me: First, if you are also mourning or having a difficult time on the day of the month of the tragedy, then change how you to treat it to something like an anniversary or birthday.

You can't just tell yourself to ignore it. If you could, you would, right? So being prepared, and surrounding yourself with people who love you is a good starting place. A second thing that helps on these days is to light a candle and write down a happy memory you have which includes the person you're grieving.

A poem written by Helen Steiner Rice is one I enjoy reading when my mind seems blank on memories. It says,

"May tender memories soften your grief.
May fond recollection bring relief.

And may you find comfort and peace in the thought
Of the joy that knowing your loved one brought...
For time and space can never divide
Or keep your loved one from your side.
When memory paints in colors true,
The happy hours that belonged to you."[1]

Even if months have passed, keep carrying your notecards on "how to respond to insensitive, rude, or ignorant questions" with you. I was not expecting people would actually think I should be over Mike, or that somehow, I could just replace him. I heard people say things like, "At least you are pretty. It shouldn't be difficult to find a new husband," or "Those kids sure could use a dad," as if Mike was replaceable. I was just coming out of shock.

I would write down the comment, then safely burn or shred them once a week. Remind yourself, these comments are coming from a place of complete ignorance. They have no clue as to what you have gone through and what you are now experiencing. If you are attending a support group, sharing these thoughtless comments to the group will usually stimulate empathetic understanding. The other members will likely report getting even more ridiculous comments. In that safe place, you can laugh together about it. Laughter is good medicine. It releases stress and stimulates healing.

If you can afford it, take your time before going back to work. You have lost a loved one and grief can linger although you may feel like you're okay. For those who enjoy staying busy, going back to work could be the best thing for you. Find what works for you. If you do have children still living at home, make sure to make new, special memories when time/money allows.

chapter nine

MILESTONES, ANNIVERSARIES, & THE HOLIDAYS

It was the start of fall and the kids were back in school. After I picked them up from school, I rushed them from grief counseling and sporting events, to home complete with dinner and bedtime routines.

Summer had been filled with beautiful distractions like trips and family time with Jordan. Once the school year hit, I was alone with my thoughts and grief would hit me in waves, sometimes to the point that I could only lay on the ground weeping. Everything I had used to keep me from facing reality was hitting me all over again. I had to really press in and remind myself every morning that, "I am NOT a victim. I am victorious."

I knew I was not quite ready to start helping rape and incest survivors as I had done before Mike's death. I knew I needed time to heal and continue doing the work of grieving. I knew in the depths of my soul, that God truly loved me. I had witnessed miracle after miracle since Mike's death. Yet, with the kids back in school, I felt like my life had lost its purpose.

My best friend/partner/husband was gone, as well as our business. I could no longer afford to counsel and coach women free of charge. I knew God created me to help others, but at the moment, I was the one needing help.

> I learned that after any tragedy, I had to allow God to heal me first.

I also had to trust that God would heal my children. They needed me as mom more than ever before, not as their counselor. We were all still going to professional grief counseling. Michael Jr.'s counselor put it best when he called himself a coach that helped people heal. At times, I think we could all use a "feelings coach".

Over the summer, the three kids and I had celebrated what would have been Mike's 46th birthday. Since this chapter covers my first fall season without Mike, I have chosen to devote the whole chapter to holidays, anniversaries, birthdays, special events, and special times of year. Fall was always my favorite time of year. Celeste and Michael were both born in November, I got married in November, and I had always hosted Thanksgiving dinner for my extended family. After Mike's death, nothing was the same. Trying to pretend or make things the same ended up causing more pain, regret, and heartache.

So to help make the journey less jarring, here are some things we did, as well as things I have learned along the way that can make these special days better.

FOR YOUR LOVED ONE'S BIRTHDAY

- **Have a plan in advance.** Even if you think you will be fine on that specific day, plan ahead.

- **Visit their favorite spot.** I took the children to Mike's favorite restaurant. It was expensive, so it was a treat to eat there. While we were there, everyone shared a favorite memory of daddy.

- **Do a balloon release.** Gather a couple close friends and family to your home. Ask each person to write down something they are having a difficult time releasing or forgiving about your loved one. For instance, you write down how angry you are that they left you with such a mess. Put that piece of paper in a helium balloon and release the balloons in the room in your home that has the highest ceilings.

- Helpful hints: Use small pieces of paper. Put the paper in the balloon first and then inflate. Third, tie those balloons to bigger, pre-purchased helium balloons (most dollar stores sell helium balloons).

  Assure everyone who is participating that what they write and put inside their balloon will stay private. Each time you see the balloons, remind yourself what you are choosing to let go of. When a balloon drifts downward, pop it, and completely dispose of it. Allow your children to pop their own balloon.

Decorate the gravesite with birthday favors. Most cemeteries allow decorations, but check with the cemetery management. They may have limits on how long decorations can be left out, or they might throw the decorations away.

Write your loved one a birthday note. Tell them what you wish they knew about you since they have been gone.

Repurpose birthday money. One year, I used the money I would have spent on Mike's birthday presents and allowed the kids to pick out a present for themselves.

RITUALS

Rituals are an important way to help you keep an enduring connection with your loved one while moving forward with life in a healthy way. I've included some examples of rituals below. You don't have to necessarily repeat the specific rituals. You might try something and find that makes you feel sad or upsets your children. Obviously, that particular ritual isn't the answer. The most important thing is that you choose something that reminds you of a happy memory and makes you feel better.

- Plant a tree in their memory.
- Watch a movie you both enjoyed together. (Do not watch it alone. Invite friends and family.) Tell them the parts of the movie your loved one thought were especially funny or good.
- Play 'your song' and share the silly or goofy things about the song that you and your loved one enjoyed. Maybe, make up a dance.

- Give a donation in honor of your loved one.
- Light a candle.
- Cook or make your loved one's favorite meal and (or) dessert.
- Visit the cemetery and just talk to them like they are sitting beside you. I have also taken reading material and sat on a nearby bench to read and meditate.
- Decorate their grave. Some cemeteries do not allow decorations, so get permission first. I took my children to a store to pick out something for their daddy that they wanted to leave for him at the cemetery. Be aware, cemeteries are not immune to theft or weather. Don't leave special or irreplaceable items at the cemetery. Don't be surprised or upset if your decorations are gone when you visit the next time.
- Volunteer. One of the best ways to honor the memory of your loved one is to get outside of your own grief and help someone else. Food shelters, animal shelters, and nursing homes can always use volunteer help. Research and arrange in advance the place where you would like to volunteer so you can honor any guidelines they have in place.
- Scrapbook or make a memory book of your loved one. This is a great thing to do with your children. The books also make a great gift for your children or someone else that had a close relationship with your loved one.
- Write down some of your loved one's favorite sayings.

> Spend these significant days with people
> you know love you and you love as well.

You will need to be the one who reaches out to friends or family. Tell them the significance the day holds. Maybe it's the anniversary of the first time you met, or your first date, or the sixth month anniversary of the day they died. If you lost your child, maybe this is the anniversary of the first time your child said "mommy" or "daddy". Tell them what you need and expect from them.

People really don't know what to say or do, even if they know you well. If you want them to share a story about your loved one, tell them in advance. Most people need a couple of days to think of something positive or funny.

CEMETERIES AND MEMORIALS

My youngest child, Michael, gets very upset when we go to the cemetery. Please, if you have children, remember they are all different and grieve in different ways. Don't try to force them to go to the gravesite if they aren't ready.

We, as a family have always gotten a rock, shell, or sand from our vacations. Recently, when I stubbed my toe on that collection of rocks, I decided they belonged in a better place. I made a small memorial for Mike in a corner of our backyard. I matched it with the other landscaping and put a little cross with a scripture on it in the middle of the rocks. Then Celeste, Michael and I put all those special rocks and shells in that area. I told the kids this was a safe place to go anytime they just wanted to talk to daddy or were especially missing him. This might be a good idea for those of you whose loved one was cremated.

SOCIAL MEDIA

There are many websites for those who have lost a loved one. I found a site specifically for widows. They actually check to make sure you have lost a loved one before you are accepted to join the site. At first, I recommended this site in my first draft of this book, but upon reflection, I am not recommending any website until you have gone through the work of healing.

There were so many wounded, hurting people with raw emotions on that site. Their comments were too descriptive of when they found their loved ones. This caused me to have flashbacks of Mike. It also brought back that gut-wrenching sorrow I experienced so intensely the first few months after Mike died. I don't want any of you to experience that until you at least have all the tools you need. Chat rooms, groups, blogs, even social media are very impersonal and not always what they appear to be representing. I have learned that people will take advantage of someone going through a tragedy. This is not the time in your life to blindly trust others. Please use wisdom.

Most importantly, getting lost on your computer for hours every day is not healthy, especially for someone trying to heal. I understand social media is a wonderful way to stay in touch with friends and family that live out of town. If the person lives in town, call them. Get together for a cup of coffee. I recommend spending no more than one hour a day on social media. (I'm obviously not referring to time you might spend at work or for your business.)

Everyone has an opinion about what you have experienced and what you should do. Remember, even on websites designed for those who have lost a loved one, even though the people on them can relate to you, they are also wounded and in need of healing. Professional grief counselors are not on these sites counseling you.

MEMORY QUILTS

At a local fabric store, you can probably get the name of a quilter who makes memory quilts. They are a wonderful way to literally wrap yourself in the memory of your loved one. Each of my children has a quilt. Michael's quilt has twelve different t-shirts ranging from sports Michael played and his daddy coached to the matching shirts they had from Disney World. Celeste and Jordan both have quilts with twelve of their favorite pictures of their daddy.

MEMORY BOOK

To my surprise, on the third year of celebrating Mike's birthday without him, Michael burst into tears when I asked him to share a memory of his daddy. I didn't understand why he was so upset. Finally, Michael shared with me that he was starting to forget memories of things he and his daddy shared. Oh, how that broke my heart! Remember Michael was only eight-years-old when his daddy died. I realized how important it was for me to immediately start a journal for each child of things they did with their dad, things he said about them, and pictures of the two of them together with the story of what was going on when the picture was taken.

Now, I have a folder for each of them containing different memories I've remembered that are specific to them and their daddy. I have also asked Celeste and Jordan to write memories they have with their daddy so they can share them with Michael. One time, I got all excited and pulled out twenty years of unorganized pictures I was going to sort through for each child. Bad idea! Start slow, and if you are going through bunches of pictures, have a close friend with you. I got so overwhelmed, all I could do was sit and get lost in the memory of each picture.

HOLIDAYS AND SIGNIFICANT DAYS

Gift-Giving Holidays

I recommend this for your biggest gift-giving holiday. Ours is Christmas. Write a letter to your loved one expressing what you would want them to know about things you have learned, accomplished, and achieved since they've been gone. Keep this letter upbeat or even funny. Tell them where you have traveled or about any new friends.

This is also a great exercise for children. Some prompts are:

- What is something you want your daddy to know about you?
- What have you done that would make your daddy proud?
- What is something new that you have started?

It's good to remind your children what they have done that their loved one would be super proud of. Of course, add that you are very proud of them also. On our first Christmas without Mike, Celeste (13, at the time) said, "I would tell daddy that I have grown five inches!"

I shared with the kids how proud daddy would be of me when our cat released a live and still flying bird into our house. I successfully recaptured the bird and released it unharmed. I never would have done that or even tried had Mike been there to rescue us from the bird invasion.

You are really giving this gift to yourself (and children). This will remind yourself how far you have come, or perhaps on how far you plan to go.

Wedding Anniversary

Do something fun and surround yourself with people you love on this special day. Our anniversary was November 25th. Of course, in 2014, that day fell two days before Thanksgiving. I knew I could not be in my home hosting Thanksgiving dinner right after my first wedding anniversary without Mike. Five months in advance, I planned to take my children to Cancun, Mexico. It was our favorite place to go, and one of our best family vacations. I wanted as much of my family to go as possible so they could be there for me on this most difficult day.

My parents, my sister and her youngest son (who was 19-years-old) were able to join us. Mike had bought me a beautiful formal dress to wear the next time we went to Mexico. I was never able to wear it for him, but I took the dress with me and planned to wear it on our anniversary night. I knew I needed to be as far away from my normal fall traditions as possible and surrounded by the love of my family.

I invited my best friend to join us. Luckily, her husband was willing to share her with me on Thanksgiving. On my anniversary day, I assumed I would be surrounded by the family I had brought with me. My best friend, my nephew, and my children had dinner with me that night. Nobody else acknowledged that day as my anniversary. It wasn't because they didn't love me. Instead of being clear on what I needed from them that day, I assumed they knew.

So, please understand your loved ones do not know what you want or need unless you clearly tell them. Anniversaries are a good time to talk to those who were in your wedding. Get together in person if possible. If you have children, pull out those wedding pictures. Have fun making jokes about the dresses or hair styles. Tell your children stories about the wedding and reception. Every wedding has a few funny stories to share. Make the day lighthearted and fun. Buy yourself flowers. This may sound selfish, but make this day about you!

Mother's Day / Father's Day

First, I will address those of you who have lost a child. If this was your only child, please know that you are still a mother or father. If you attend a church, know in advance they will probably speak on motherhood/fatherhood. If they ask all the mothers / fathers to stand up for recognition, that is you! So, stand!

This is a great day to cook your child's favorite meal. If you decide to go through pictures, I would strongly recommend having someone there with you. Sitting alone surrounded by a pile of pictures of the child that is no longer with you can be very overwhelming and depressing.

If you lost your spouse and you have children, understand that these two days have changed forever. I will call these days, "Your Day" i.e. my day is "Mother's Day", and call the other holiday "Your Loved One's Day". On "Your Day", depending on the ages of your children, have a friend take them shopping to get you something special. Sometimes children get upset because they want to give you something nice and do not have money or a way to go shopping for you.

Mike always went overboard on Mother's Day with gifts and flowers. My children wanted to continue that tradition even though I just wanted something homemade. This was important to them and they wanted it to continue. I would not have thought about how important it was to them had it not been for my best friend taking the kids shopping and paying for the gifts they picked out. I noticed how proud Celeste was when she saw me using and enjoying the gift she had selected for me. Keep this in mind when "Your Day" occurs and all you want to do is cover your head and sleep.

Our first "Your Loved One's Day" was Father's Day without Mike. We went to church but I quickly realized that going to church on this day and hearing the majority of the topic be about a father my children no longer had was just too much grief. For now, I have chosen for us not to attend church on this day. If you do go, be prepared and be with additional family, not just your children.

Regardless of where you go, your children are aware of what day it is. I pulled out some pictures I had taken on past Father's Days and we laughed. Pictures are a great way to strengthen memories in younger children who might start forgetting some of the loving details of the lost parent.

This is another great time to make a favorite meal or dessert of your loved one. Talk about some of the children's favorite gifts they gave their loved one and why. I also liked to tell the children what their daddy really loved about each one of them.

Christmas

This was our big holiday. We usually stayed at our house and Mike made it so very special. On Christmas Eve, we would go to church and then enjoy a Swedish meal with extended family. When a holiday comes around that has deep family traditions, I would strongly suggest doing something completely different and fun. For our first Christmas without Mike, we went to Arkansas to be with my sister and my two nephews.

I will caution you from my own painful experience: Do not over spend on presents and gifts trying to make up for the fact that their loved one is no longer alive. All that does is put you in debt. There is no amount of money or gifts that can make a child forget their parent is not there.

New Year's Eve / Day

Because my children were young at the time, this was not a very big holiday for us yet. I still suggest not being alone. Plan ahead just like any other special holiday. Maybe, do something you always wanted to do but your loved one never wanted to do it. You know what holidays are special to you and your children, so plan, plan, plan! I cannot express that enough. Planning gives you special things to look forward to. Mark these special events on a "family" calendar!

Anniversary of the Death

Most people, even other family members not living in the home, will probably not remember this date or realize its meaning to you and your children. If the death occurred near a holiday, be aware that your children might associate their deep loss and sorrow with that holiday.

Mike died on February 12, 2014, two days before Valentine's Day and the big school class party. In 2015, I remember Michael (who was nine-years-old) saying, "I hate Valentine's Day and I will never celebrate it!" I felt so sad that he associated Valentine's Day with death and the loss of his daddy. Be aware of those holidays and always check in with your children.

Regardless of whether you feel like it won't be different than any other day or not, it will be difficult. If your loved one died where you are still living, I would recommend that you and your children spend the night at a friend's or family member's house. Get out of the environment where you were the year before when you found your loved one. There are really fun hotels that have indoor swimming parks. Whatever you do, join in and play with your children. Make new memories that are fun and happy.

For school, I gave my children a choice if they wanted to go or not. Michael chose to stay home and Celeste decided to go. That night, we went to a fun store with the kids' godparents and two of their daughters. We finished the evening with dinner together. We told funny stories about Mike and kept the mood happy. Children love embarrassing stories about you and your loved one.

Ask your children if they have any questions about their loved one. Try to keep focused on positive memories. If you can, do something you enjoy like a massage, a facial, or a round of golf. Take time to really enjoy yourself. Look back over the last year. Be proud of all you have learned. Remember something new you've done especially if you never thought you could do it. Or, just be proud you survived the first year. Take time to give yourself a pat on the back.

Military Holidays

If your loved one served in the military, you may have mixed emotions about their service especially if you feel let down by the military or VA. Veteran's Day, Memorial Day, and other holidays designed to honor those who bravely served in our military might trigger anger. Any anger allowed to remain will eventually turn into bitterness. Blaming the military was only hurting me, so I chose to forgive.

On Veteran's Day, my church honored all those who served our country and their spouses. I had forgotten this tradition, so this totally caught me off guard. I sat in my chair at church crying alone, thinking about the year prior when I stood proudly by my husband as he was honored. It was a huge reminder that life, as well as much of my identity, had forever changed. It was a good opportunity for me to talk to my children about their father's great service to our country, and allow them to see me grieve. I'm not sure my running out of church crying was the healthiest thing for my children to witness, but it reminded them that grief will come in waves. Something arbitrary might come up that reminds them of how much they loved their daddy and how much they miss him. By my imperfect example, they learned it is always okay to feel and deal with that grief.

Special Days

You must be the one who reaches out!

Be around people who love you and want to be there for you. Understand that sometimes friends and family want the 'old' us back, not realizing 'we' can't ever offer that again. The last thing people around us want to think is that we might still be grieving. Many people mistakenly believe that it's better not to talk about 'it', because that would only make things worse. I often have to remind people close to us to please bring Mike up in funny, inspiring, and uplifting stories.

Remember your loved ones are trying to protect you, although they might really be protecting themselves. Encourage those close to you to use the name of the loved one you lost and give them grace.

SITUATIONS TO BE MINDFUL OF WITH GRIEVING CHILDREN

Many events will come up at school and other places. Remember, our first Christmas after was with my sister, my nephews, and my parents. We attended my sister's church on Christmas Eve to hear the Christmas Story and sing Christmas songs. What could possibly go wrong? Well, an adorable baby was learning to say "daddy" for the first time. This innocent scene became a great example of "expect the unexpected".

Over and over, the baby said, "Da-da, dada, daddy."

I looked over to Michael Jr., who was sitting directly in front of the baby. Tears were streaming down his face. I was crushed. I didn't hear another word of the Christmas story. I held Michael tightly and told him how much I loved him. Thinking back, I wish I had taken Michael out into the lobby and used that time to discuss happy holiday memories.

Events at School:

- Donuts with Dad
- Muffins with Mom
- Dads of Grade schoolers
- Field Trips
- Father-Daughter Dance
- Mother-Son Events

The list of events that could trigger grief seems to go on forever. First, talk to your children and get their feedback on the upcoming event. Second, use the buddy system. Have an adult friend join you. Even on school field trips, if you talk to the teacher, they will usually allow you to buddy up with another parent that is your friend. If it's a Father-Daughter Dance and your daughter does not want to attend with an uncle, family friend, or grandpa, then try a special 'date' night with just you and her.

I started volunteering at school on those 'Special Parent' days. If the kids wanted to attend, my parents would take them so they could show them their classrooms, artwork, and other important stuff. If they absolutely did not want to go, I would take them somewhere fun for breakfast. Remember, you are only one person. Don't try being both mom and dad.

The key for success at these types of events is to know that you are bound to run into at least one or two people that do not know your loved one has died so be prepared. Have your children prepared also.

You all will be asked, "Where's your dad/ mom/spouse?"

Then, of course, the questions will start. "What happened? Why? How?"

I taught my children to respond with, "He died, and it's personal to my family. Thank you for asking," or "He died, please keep us in your prayers."

Then I told them to politely walk away. I have taught my children that if someone attempts to persist with questions, to tell them they can talk to me. Since that person is being extremely rude, chances are they will not pursue questions with an adult. Someone asking questions who wasn't a friend and was being rude, just wants gossip.

I say, "It has been a very difficult time. If you want to help, you can donate money for flowers."

I don't care how long it has been since Mike's death. I just care that my response usually shuts the person up.

chapter ten

HOW COULD GOD ASK ME TO DO THIS?

We made it through our first Christmas without Mike. On December 27th, 2014, Celeste, Michael and I loaded all our stuff into the minivan and left Jonesboro, Arkansas. The drive back to Missouri was about seven to eight hours. It was later in the evening and both kids readily fell asleep. While driving, I listened to a preacher to keep my mind focused on good things.

Suddenly, I saw a very clear picture of a woman, perhaps she had been a bartender or maybe Mike's waitress. I saw her face so clearly, I could have drawn it. She was pretty and had long hair, but her face looked worn-down like life had been difficult.

I heard that whisper say, "Shawna, I want you to go into that bar and tell her that Mike took his life later that night. Share Me, and tell her that I love her."

This broke my heart, not because I wanted to sue the bar, (even though I could have really used the money) but because it was the worst place in the entire world I could think of walking into. My heart felt sick at the thought of going into that dark, horrible bar. My husband got extremely drunk there, yet no one stopped him or cut him off.

I knew this was the last place Mike had been because I had the receipt. Those were the last filthy, dark walls Mike saw before somehow getting home. When he drank, he talked to anyone and everyone. I knew those were the last people he spoke to. Still nobody even thought to drive him home. I'm relieved Mike didn't hit any innocent people while driving that night. After all I had been through over these last ten months, how could God really ask me to go there?

I argued with God and I begged Him not to ask me go into that bar. I could not even drive by it without feeling sick to my stomach. How was I supposed to walk in? I promised God I would forgive the waitress, the owner of the bar, and anyone else that had been in the bar that night. I then begged Him, "Just please, please don't ask me go into that bar." Anywhere but there. Anything but that!

"Please don't ask me to share about You or what happened later that night," I pleaded.

But God kept showing me the woman's face during this long drive home. I kept wrestling with God for the next forty-five minutes, maybe longer. I would try thinking about something else. I even listened to different music, yet I still saw her face. As I studied her face in my mind, some of her deep wrinkles softened as if to show me what would happen as a result of my obedience.

SURRENDER

Finally, I surrendered and told God, "I will do what You want—whatever You want."

As soon as I said that, tears started streaming down my face. I had no idea how I was going to get the courage to do what God was asking of me, but I was going to do it.

As I drove the rest of the way home, I mentally rehearsed some ways I knew would help me extend forgiveness to those at the bar I viewed as complicit in his death. Through my ministry to help rape and incest victims, I taught women all about forgiveness, what it is and is NOT, and ways to extend forgiveness. Now I was the one that needed to extend my forgiveness to those I felt had hurt me. The people at the bar had no idea I even existed. I learned firsthand (the hard way) the importance of forgiveness.

> "Unforgiveness is a prison. When you choose to forgive, the person you set free is yourself." – unknown

I'm not sure where I heard this saying, but I found it to be true. I also found it is much easier to say than to actually do, especially when your life has been shattered. Forgiveness is a choice. If you are waiting to 'feel' like forgiving, you probably won't. If you are waiting for the people that hurt you to apologize, you may have a very long wait ahead of you. The person you need to forgive might be your deceased loved one.

The first person I recommend you forgive is yourself. Forgiveness, like healing, is a choice you must make. Don't allow your wounds to turn into unforgiveness and ultimately bitterness. In the "What Helped" section of this chapter, I share some things that can help you understand forgiveness better and steps to extend forgiveness to others.

I forgave everyone from the bar I could think of hoping that if I did, God wouldn't make me go there. Alas, He continued to lay on my heart the importance of going there and sharing Him and His love. I still wondered why God would show me this woman's face so clearly and ask me to go into that bar.

"There are so many people better equipped to share His love than me," I thought.

It felt like I was being asked to dig up my husband's grave every time I even thought about going. I had to make a choice; was I going to obey God and trust in the One who had supplied all my needs over the last year or not? Of course, I was going to obey.

There were a few other details about my trip to this bar that I needed to get in order before I went. I heard in my spirit that I needed to make two color copies of our last family photo. I also needed to purchase two Bibles. Then I was to take the two pictures and glue them to the first page on each of the Bibles. The final thing I was to do was highlight Psalms 68:5 in both Bibles. Psalms 68:5 NIV says, "A father [God] to the fatherless, a defender of widows, is God in His holy dwelling."

I didn't understand why God would want me to highlight that specific verse in Psalms. It seemed like there were so many other verses in the Bible to share Jesus' love with someone. Despite my lack of understanding it all, I did everything God asked me to do before going to the bar.

THE DAY HAD COME

I picked a day and time about three weeks away—January 16th, 2015. That day finally arrived. That morning, it occurred to me that before I show up at 2 o'clock in the afternoon, I should make sure the bar was even open so early in the day.

I drove into the bar parking lot and asked God to use me however He wanted. Knowing God sent me there; I surrendered everything in me and trusted He would give me the words to say. After I finished praying, I was about to leave when a Camaro drove by me. It was just like the Camaro Brighton saw in his vision. It was Mike's dream car! I had lived in my city for years and never saw a car specifically like this one. Here it was driving by me. This was a sign from God. It reassured me I was doing what He told me to do.

I was so nervous. I really wasn't sure if they were going to kick me out of the bar or what else would happen. I thought I was going into this bar to 'extend my forgiveness' to the owner and the waitress that served Mike the night he took his life. I had assumed the face God had so clearly shown me just weeks before was that waitress. I also assumed I was there to share that God loved them and assure them that I was not going to sue them.

The bar was packed with people, which was surprising since it was the middle of the afternoon. As I looked around, I only saw one person, a bartender, who looked like they were working. As I walked toward the bar, she turned around. I felt weak in my knees and in complete awe because this was the woman I was seeing in my head for the last three weeks. I was so excited. There she stood with her long hair, working very hard in a packed bar. I was absolutely positive she was the women I was supposed to talk with.

I must have looked like a deer in the headlights as I just stared at her. She walked over to me and asked if I was there to fundraise for an organization. Apparently, I did not look like I was there to drink. I asked if I could talk to her and the owner of the bar. Again, I had assumed that since God had told me to buy two Bibles I was supposed to speak to the women God showed me and the owner. After all, I was informing them that I had no intentions on suing the bar.

She said something like, "The owner won't be in for hours and I'm the only person running the whole bar."

I asked, "Could I have just fifteen minutes of your time to speak to you?"

"It would be at least twenty to thirty minutes before I could get away. I'm so busy," she said.

"I would be glad to wait and I only need maybe ten minutes," I said. Then, I asked, "Would it be alright if I waited even if it was a long wait?"

"Sure," she said.

She was so busy she couldn't even take a bathroom break. I knew I was there to speak with her, so I sat on the one empty bar stool and waited while I wondered why God had me bring two Bibles. Was I wrong?

NOT INTERESTED

After waiting for what seemed like hours, (only forty-five minutes), every person in the bar either had a full drink or had left. While I waited, I asked God if perhaps I was there on the wrong day or wrong time. The owner wasn't even there. The bartender could finally give me about five minutes of her time, so I wanted to respect that limit. I thanked her for her time and assured her I was there for a purpose.

As I got Mike's bar receipt out to show her, I said, "My name is Shawna Mertel."

It had been almost a year since Mike had been there.

I said, "My husband got very drunk at this bar that night, much more than I had ever seen him before. Later that same night, he took his own life."

I reassured her that I had no intentions of suing the bar. Before I could continue, she wanted to look at the receipt. She never worked on Wednesdays, plus the receipt had the server's number on it for identification. We were both positive, she was not the person who served Mike that night. In fact, she wasn't even at the bar that night. I went ahead and shared with her that Jesus Christ came to earth, lived a perfect life and then willingly died for all our mistakes and sins so that we could have a personal relationship with God. I could see she wasn't really interested in what I was saying.

In my mind, I questioned, "What in the world am I doing at this bar when the owner and Mike's server both are not even here?"

It didn't feel like anything was going the way I thought it was supposed to go. Gently, God reminded me that this was the women He showed me. This was who God wanted me to share my story with. God wanted her to know how much He loved her. I didn't know what else to do, so I told her about the vision I had of her face, and that she was, without a doubt, the one God wanted me to talk to.

Just then I heard another whisper from God saying, "What did I tell you to say?"

In my head, I said," You told me to tell her how much You love her."

I realized it was God, the Father, wanting me to tell her how much He loved her, that He would go to the ends of the earth, just to tell her He loved her, that she was worth dying for, that she is His precious daughter and He wanted to be her daddy!

> I recomposed myself right in front of this woman and I looked at her face with the full understanding of why God sent me there—it was for her.

SIMILAR SCARS

I got out one of the Bibles I had brought and I opened it to the picture of my beautiful family. I pointed to my children and said, "You know, my children lost their daddy almost a year ago, on February 12, 2014, but they did not lose their heavenly daddy, and He would never let them down."

I showed her Psalm 68:5, and read out loud the part that said, "God is a father to the fatherless." I stopped, looked her in the eyes and told her that God had been showing me her face as clear as I was seeing it now since December 27th. I shared with her how God had told me that He wanted to be her daddy. He is her heavenly Father, and knows all her pain and her heartache, and He loves her with an everlasting, perfect love.

I said, "God asked me to come into the worst, darkest place I could imagine walking into because God loves you so much."

God wanted her to know that even though she thought churches were just buildings filled with hypocrites, His love for her was not limited by manmade walls. God sent someone into this bar just to tell her that she is loved. Her eyes began to fill with tears as I gave her the Bible.

I said, "God gave my kids huge hearts for other children who are fatherless. God can comfort anyone that has lost a parent."

Through her tears she said, "I haven't told anyone really, but last month my dad committed suicide."

I was stunned! My mind flooded with a deeper understanding of God's love for us. My heart overflowed with forgiveness for the bar owner, the waitress, and anyone else that I had blamed. I did not have to force forgiveness anymore. I knew I would no longer feel sick to my stomach when I drove by the bar. I wasn't there to extend "my forgiveness" or to inform the owner I wasn't going to sue him, I was there because God wanted me to tell His child how much He loves her.

He saw every tear and knew the deep longing she had for a father. She hugged me and we prayed together. She couldn't believe God cared so much He sent me there just for her. The God of the universe cared enough for both of us to send me to share His love. I understood her pain. This reminded me God is so much bigger than we could ever imagine. It was about Him and His great love reaching out to a woman who had been recently shattered by suicide.

> There is no place on earth you can go to hide from God's love. It is a free gift, but like all gifts, it is your choice to receive it.

(If you would like to receive this free gift of love, all it takes is a simple prayer you can pray right now asking God to reveal Himself to you.)

The bartender asked, "Do you have another Bible?"

Of course, I did.

I said, "God actually told me to bring two Bibles."

She said, "I don't have a Bible at home and would love another one for my children."

I grabbed the second Bible and showed her they both had a picture of my family in them and the same verse highlighted.

I said, "God loves you so much that He had the least likely person—me—a widow, whose husband committed suicide, to share His love and heart with you."

God will never cease to amaze me. He heals the broken hearted.

WHAT HELPED

Forgiveness is key. If you truly want to experience joy and healing, you must go through the process of forgiveness. When you choose to forgive, you release yourself from what or who hurt you. Forgiveness is a choice. It's *your* choice. It's not a feeling. "Forgive and forget" is not a reality. If it was, we would just forget the tragedy we've been through. Forgiveness is not pretending the horrible event hasn't occurred or in any way condoning an unacceptable action.

Forgiving someone does not mean blindly trusting them. Trust must be rebuilt. Often, that is not possible when forgiving someone who has died. By forgiving, we are surrendering our right to 'get even'.

Start by forgiving yourself. Whether it's things you have done, said, or thought about that make you feel shame or "at fault", say out loud, "God, I choose to forgive myself for my mistakes, faults, and failings either real or perceived. Just as you have forgiven me of all my mistakes and don't hold them against me, today, I forgive myself."

Know that God does NOT ever plan, will or desire someone to take their own life. Often, we blame God for our tragedy. To top off our pain, many of us have heard some well meaning people tell us that our tragedy is somehow "God's will" or "His plan". Let me assure you of one thing I absolutely know, this breaks His heart.

It is true that God knows everything that will ever happen to us. Yet in His love for us, He gave us freewill. Sometimes that freewill allows others to do things that shatter our world. God is not able to sin [make mistakes] but we still blame Him. Here is an example of a prayer you might want to use if you have found yourself blaming God or resenting Him for what you have gone through:

"Dear God, I choose to forgive You for what I thought was your punishment when tragedy came into my life. I became angry and resentful of You. Please forgive me of this wrong thinking and heal my mind and heart today."

Practice the "Steps to Forgiveness". *(Handout from Remuda Ranch Center)*

a. Choose to forgive the hurt. Remember, it is not a feeling. It is a decision. I did this by praying for the person who hurt me every time I remembered how they hurt me. It took over a year before I was actually angry at Mike for taking his life. I blamed the military and anyone else I thought contributed to his suicide. The bottom line is he chose to drink alcohol to the point he no longer made clear decisions and then chose to shoot himself. Nobody else made those decisions for him.

When forgiving someone who is dead, I've found that praying for God to release the anger, hurt, and sadness in me works best since praying for him is no longer beneficial. I did pray that God would not hold the hurt Mike caused me against him.

b. When the people you are forgiving are still living, remember you are forgiving the hurt and pain they have caused you, not allowing them to continue to hurt you. You need to protect yourself and your children from any additional pain or hurt. This may include taking official action. If they have broken the law, forgiveness does not mean they don't need to be turned into the proper authorities. Allowing that person to continue to hurt you or others is not forgiveness, it's denial and enabling.

c. Identify the person who caused the problem and the consequences of that hurt. Acknowledge they have caused you real pain, perhaps a life-altering trauma or tragedy, and you are *choosing* forgiveness. The pain will not magically disappear, but you will break the chains that hold you to that pain. Sometimes it's an organization, or place that caused you pain. Treat it the same as you would an individual. (For example, I was very angry and blamed the military.)

d. Do not wait for the person or organization to seek your forgiveness. Of course, when you're forgiving someone who is dead, they obviously cannot ask you to forgive them. Often, the offender won't admit their fault, even after you have forgiven them. (The man who sexually abused me never admitted fault, even from prison, yet I am so thankful I released myself from the prison of unforgiveness.) However, it is wonderful when the person who hurt you realizes their mistake and seeks forgiveness from you. Don't hold your breath; be the one who forgives first.

Pick a day of the week to pray for those whom you decide to forgive. I selected Friday, so I call it, 'Forgiving Friday'. When I first started praying for the person that hurt me, it sounded more like a plea for God to help me forgive them. As I healed, I was able to pray for God to bless them. My 'test' to take them off my Friday list was if and when I heard that person was blessed, I could truly feel happy for them. I prayed for one person for over eight years!

CONCLUSION

If you've made it this far through the book, you are equipped with amazing tools and strategies to continue on your healing journey. Remember to go over the 'What Helped' sections regularly to remind yourself of what still needs work or what steps you might need to repeat.

Grief seems to come in waves. When you have a new event, prepare in advance using some of the tools you've gained.

VICTORY JOURNAL

Keep a Victory Journal where you write down stuff you never thought you could or would ever do. Here's a sample entry from mine:

> *Yesterday, I put a bicycle chain on my son's bike for the very first time in my life.*

In my journal, there are things like:

- bought my first car

- drove across the country with my children (over 3000 miles) two separate summers
- balanced a checkbook
- doing the finances
- bought Michael his first 'big boy bike'
- took my family to another country (twice!)
- dealt with insurance and contractors on a flooded basement
- captured a wild bird that flew in my home and released it safely back to the wild
- bought my first computer
- taught Celeste how to drive

Sure, some could be considered embarrassing. You may be wondering, "How could someone in their late forties not know how to do these things?" etc. Instead of giving any space to that condemning voice in my head, I write what I've done so I remind myself that I have made incredible progress. I'm strong and getting stronger! Whatever the new thing is, I'm learning how to do it now. And for that, I am proud.

> On days I feel like I haven't done or cannot do anything right; I look in my Victory Journal and see all the things I have learned.

If you lost a child, your Victory Journal could be done from one of these approaches:

(Remember, the key is to keep a record of your successes as you are growing and learning to live without your loved one by your side.)

a. What you are able to do now that maybe you couldn't do when your child first died.

b. What you would be teaching your child at the age they would currently be. If they would be around the age where you would be teaching them to drive, volunteer to help a friend teach their teenager to drive. Trust me, they'll appreciate the help. Volunteer at a school. Even colleges could use volunteers.

NEEDS CHANGE OVER TIME

I remember 'graduating' from grief group with Michael. I really thought, "Wow, I'm glad that's over". The group had a little good-bye ceremony for us. Things were good, but grief had not disappeared. At that time, we had reached a place where the group was not helping us move forward so we took a break. Returning to the grief group later was not a sign of failure, just an acknowledgement that as life changed, our needs also changed. For example, during times of a higher grief load where we thought about Mike more (like during the month of February, the anniversary of Mike's death), I increased our individual counseling sessions.

> As children grow physically, they also grow mentally, which means they process death differently as their understanding increases.

GRIEF DOESN'T FOLLOW A SCHEDULE

Some might think that grief hits hardest immediately following tragedy but that isn't always the case. Grief sometimes shows up when it is least expected. It doesn't have a schedule or a predictable timeline you can refer to. You have to keep your eyes and ears open to what is going on in the lives of your children. Since it is often difficult to see your own behavior, it is important to have a trusted friend or two who can speak honestly to you about any concerning observation of your wellbeing.

Here are a few examples of grief timelines and triggers we experienced:

- It took at least a year and a half before I could admit I was angry at Mike for leaving us with such a huge mess!

- Celeste's first day of high school (over two years after Mike's death), was extremely difficult. Her daddy was always her protector and he wasn't there. She had her first boyfriend, school dances, all the things her daddy joked about, (i.e. not ever letting a boy take her out or she wasn't leaving the house until she was thirty). He wasn't there for these big life changes.

- Nearly three years after Mike took his life, Michael started to blame himself (survivor's guilt). Celeste and I had already gone through survivor's guilt and understood there was nothing we could have done differently to stop Mike from taking his life.

- Three years after Mike's death, several things happened in Celeste's life (normal teenage growing up stuff), but with her daddy not there, sadness turned to depression, which then developed into clinical depression.

I was helping Michael deal with his clinical depression when I observed Celeste also behaving as if depressed. Here I was, in the middle of writing this book to help others, and found myself needing to care for two clinically depressed children. I decided to include this for several reasons:

First, remember you are doing your very best under life-shattering circumstances. Even doing everything you think is best for your children, you can never bring back the one person they lost.

Second, as children grow mentally, they are able to experience more grief which means they are able to heal more wounds. Consider it a good thing. Dealing with the grief as it comes up will teach you and especially your children how to better deal with problems as they arise throughout life.

Third, I want you to be aware of some of the possible signals indicating your children are grieving at a new level and need additional help. Michael started feeling down, and trusted people told me he wasn't like himself. He did not like going to individual counseling because it brought up sad things. Like all of us, he did not want to think about them. (Most kids will resist counseling.)

Michael did not know what was going on inside himself (as far as feeling differently/ depressed). He just couldn't get motivated to do the things he normally liked doing. I took him to his physician thinking maybe he had mononucleosis. His doctor ruled out all physical causes and said Michael was depressed. It didn't look like what 'adult' depression looked like so I was glad I had taken him to the doctor. For my eleven-year-old boy, depression looked like laziness, and a complete unwillingness to discuss his dad.

> Had I not been aware of what childhood depression looked like, it would have been easy to become frustrated with him, perhaps even punish him for not doing his chores and other things he was supposed to do.

I took him back to individual grief counseling. He slowly opened up to me and his counselor about survivor's guilt, fear of me dying, and anger that his daddy was not around to teach him and play with him. After Michael had the courage to share what he had buried deep inside, his counselor was able to help Michael grieve through them in a healthy way. I was able to offer encouragement, and reassurance.

Opening up and talking about these issues was the path to Michael healing in a healthy way. Within two weeks, the clinical depression was completely gone. Of course, new things still come up. When he is ready to grieve, we give him the support he needs to do so. Appendix B has the Developmental Stages of Children Dealing with Grief. After this eye-opening experience, I thought somehow I had failed Michael. Why was he getting depressed now? As I got him help, I found these stages and noticed that what Michael was now grieving was completely normal for his age.

When he was eight years old, his brain lacked the ability to comprehend death the same as when he was eleven. Keeping his emotions bottled up inside turned into clinical depression. Michael, thinking that these new emotions would disappoint me, or worry me that I failed, likely contributed to him not wanting to open up with what he was feeling. Once I had a better understanding, I was able to convey to him that it was very normal for him to now be worried I might die, etc. At that time, doctors wanted to put him on an antidepressant immediately. I didn't agree especially since he was only eleven. We adjusted his diet, increased his exercise, and incorporated the use of pure essential oils to help him sleep better and elevate his overall mood.

When Celeste was diagnosed with depression, her doctor was ready to put her on antidepressants even before blood work was taken. This was a major red flag for me. At that stage in development, I knew if I could work with the counselor, and the kids would be honest about their feelings, the depression would go away. One contributing factor I could easily remedy myself. Celeste was low in a few vitamins and minerals.

I am not saying that antidepressants should never be used, but I am saying that all other options and support should be tried first, especially when dealing with children and teens. Practical things like improving their diet to include healthier fuels and less junk, adding more regular exercise, increasing their vitamins and possibly adding in the use of essential oils are options that come with no negative side effects.

I can say from experience, that these things have worked miracles with my children. Michael is no longer depressed at all and sees his grief counselor once every three weeks or so. Celeste has come out of the deep depression and still sees her counselor every other week. She is exercising more and back to dancing which is one of her loves.

> Do not feel like a failure if you have to take a couple steps back. Remember you are on a journey and as long as you don't give up, you have won!

CONTINUE YOUR HEALING JOURNEY

You have chosen victory and not victimhood. You have started the hard work of healing. Please, continue your healing journey. Your life was shattered yet you decided to allow light to shine through your cracks. I wish I could give you a diploma and say, "Congratulations, you are healed!" Wouldn't that be great? Then we could all just resume living the life we once held so dear. Unfortunately, that's not how life or grief works.

You must continue improving, growing, learning, and living. The same with the tremendous grief you have experienced. Sometimes that grief destroys families, even children. Children of a parent who committed suicide are 70 percent more likely to commit suicide. So, stay committed to healing and assisting your children in their healing journey.

You wouldn't go to a gym, workout really hard for one hour then leave that gym and say, "I sure am glad I'm in shape now and never have to do that again." That would be ridiculous. But we often do that to our healing journey. That would mean turning our emotions off. If we stop feeling, the pain may briefly stop, but that would also mean we would stop feeling joy, hope, peace, and ultimately love. Life without love and emotions would not be much of a life.

PAY IT FORWARD

One of the things my basketball coach from junior and senior high school said was, "You really haven't learned something well until you can successfully teach someone else." You may not be able to acknowledge it yet, but you have already grown so much just in the time and effort you have put into reading this book. When opportunities arise, you can use your tragedy to help someone else have triumph. I look forward to hearing how you did!

Continue writing in your journals. As you continue to heal, write down those new ways you have learned to enjoy life again. I saw this poem posted by an unknown author,

> *"Grief never ends...but it changes.*
> *It's a passage, not a place to stay.*
> *Grief is not a sign of weakness or a lack of faith*
> *...it is the price of LOVE."* [1]

I would not wish one tear away if it meant I never would have known and loved my husband. As your healing grows, more and more of your cracks will go from dark and broken to shining brightly. Let them! They will draw joy and love to your life. I love watching the stars at night. The darkest time is just before dawn. It seems like the darkest time of night would be in the middle of the night, when you feel completely surrounded by the darkness, but rest assured in all God's wisdom He made the darkest time during the night to be just before the beautiful sunrise. You are so close to your sunrise.

NOTHING IS WASTED

Enjoy the life God has placed around you. Create the life you have always wanted and dreamed of. Eventually, you will start seeing your new life come into greater focus ahead of you. Maybe, your dream will become a life you never could have imagined before. Look forward to a life filled with peace, joy, and love.

At the beginning of this book, I wrote that none of our tears are wasted. Even as I typed in these words, I thought about the blood vessel that runs from my right eye to my hair line that ruptured during those first two to three months from crying so hard. It is permanent so far. The immediate blood in my eye cleared up but that vein remains a blue line from my eye to my hairline.

Were my tears wasted?

No.

Could God really use me, with all my brokenness, to help others heal from the indescribable pain of this type of loss?

My answer is, YES!

> In those times when everything within me felt completely ripped out, when my tears streamed so hard that I burst that vein, is when Jesus Christ, the Lord of my life showed Himself the most.

He shattered every preconceived idea I had about who He was or what He could do. God created you to be in relationship with Him, and nothing on earth will ever fill the space in your life that

God designed just for Him. He loves you just the way you are. You don't have to clean yourself up before you go to Him. God is the true Healer. He created our hearts and knows exactly how to heal them. Give Him your heart and He will heal it, I promise.

BEAUTY FROM ASHES

I found something I wrote in 1998 while hiking Mount St. Helens in Washington State. Mount St. Helens is one of many volcanic mountains located on the Cascade Mountain Range from northern Washington State through Oregon and Northern California. It erupted May 18, 1980.

This eruption was like an explosion akin to fifty large ocean freighters full of TNT going off at once, more than 500 times more powerful than the Hiroshima bomb. One-and-a-half cubic miles of the north face of the mountain had been pulverized. The explosion created its own atmosphere including lightning and thunder. Glaciers melted and lakes joined with explosive pumice as a wall of molten liquid raced down the valley, destroying everything in its path. Six miles surrounding the mountain were left untouched by man to study how nature would rebuild.

Mount St. Helens is an awesome beauty which brought me to my knees every time I went there to hike. On this particular day in 1998, eighteen years after the eruption, I found myself stunned with the majesty the mountain displayed.

I wrote:

> *"Mount St. Helens—so beautiful and majestic, yet completely destroyed. God in all His wisdom did not pick up the broken pieces and put the mountain back together. He*

*used the destruction to display His power and His awesome
beauty. God created something new, even more majestic and
beautiful than before.*

*My life, so much greater to God, feels destroyed like the
mountain. God will not pick up the broken pieces of my
life and put them neatly back together. No… through my
destruction, through my brokenness, He will display His
beauty and His power."*

I have witnessed His power as He shattered my theological beliefs,
and I have seen His beauty shine through my broken cracks.

> *"…He will give a crown of beauty for ashes, a joyous
> blessing instead of mourning, festive praise instead of
> despair."* (Isaiah 61:3 NLT)

This is what God wants to do for you.

I have shared the most intimate details of my life with you so
you can see all of my brokenness and all of my cracks. Yet, woven
throughout my story, was God—bigger than all my shame and
hurt, wanting to shine through me, to heal every shattered wound
suicide left in its wake.

He wants this for you, too.

I pray that as you heal, you will allow God's love, peace, and joy to
now shine out of you. You are uniquely positioned to help others
who have also been shattered. Continue on your journey of healing
and celebrate each victory along the way.

ABOUT THE AUTHOR

Shawna Mertel has a passion to help others live an extraordinary life filled with joy and love. Being filled with sexual abuse-related shame for most of her early life, she turned to an eating disorder to numb her pain. Through counselling and research, Shawna found strategies and truths to be able to live her best life. As a result of the life-changing experiences she had in healing past wounds, she began coaching and helping hundreds of women heal from childhood sexual abuse, rape and/or eating disorders.

Then, in 2014, Shawna's world was shattered into a million pieces. Her husband unexpectedly took his own life. Her love was gone, their family's business was gone, and her joy was gone. Realizing she couldn't remain a victim of choices she didn't make, she refused to waste any more time in shame and broken from grief.

Discovering there were few resources that could adequately help her or anyone else navigate this new reality as a survivor of a loved one's suicide, Shawna was determined to help others by sharing transformative healing strategies as well as helpful guidelines on how to walk through the overwhelming process of life in the aftermath.

Shawna knew she wasn't alone in the repercussions. Her children would also need their own care. She shares the importance of each child getting age-appropriate support as they heal as well as what each age milestone may encounter as their understanding and awareness expands.

Even though it was not a perfect journey, light now shines out of those shattered places in her life and joy has returned. Shawna openly shares her heartfelt journey with you so that you too can find joy again and allow love to return as you choose to heal and live life again.

www.shawnamertel.com

CONNECT WITH SHAWNA

For information regarding individual or group support and coaching, email: shawnamertel@gmail.com.

Facebook – shawnamertelinc

We are part of a family, (as with all families, we didn't choose this one) and we share a terrible tragedy, but we also share a strength and empathy that few have. You are in my heart and my prayers,

Love,

Shawna

APPENDIX A
COMMON WAYS PEOPLE REACT DURING GRIEF
(From www.kchospice.org)[1]

Changes in Mental Functioning

Inability to focus • Difficulty making decisions • Difficulty processing information • Disorganization • Difficulties with memory • Preoccupation with the deceased • Fear of "losing your mind"

Physical Responses

Change in appetite • Shortness of breath • Deep sighing • Tightness in throat • Lowered resistance to illness • Stomach problems • Increased sensitivity to noise • Sleep disturbance • Headaches • Weakness • Tight Muscles • Fatigue • Trembling • Dizziness

While these symptoms are often considered normal, it is also a good idea for a person who is grieving to consult with their physician if these symptoms are concerning.

Emotional Responses

Numbness • Anger • Bitterness • Feeling lost • Anxiety • Desire to run away • Sadness • Loneliness • Emptiness • Depression • Relief • Guilt • Yearning • Apathy • Regret • Confusion

Behavioral Responses

Crying or sobbing • Talking to your loved one • Looking for loved one • Feeling the presence of the deceased • Vivid dreams related to the loss • Restless over-activity • Decrease in productivity • Carrying objects or wearing clothing that belongs to the deceased • Difficulty engaging in self-care • Easily distracted

Social Responses

Avoiding places where memories are strong • Visiting places that hold memories of the deceased • Withdrawing from social activities • Over-engaging socially • Feeling uncomfortable in social situations • Preoccupation with health and well-being of your loved ones • Avoiding friends and family • Being easily distracted

Spiritual Responses

Anger that prayers were not answered • Sense of abandonment or punishment at a time of deepest need

• Questioning "Why?" or "Why now?" • Loss of meaning or purpose • Searching for meaning and purpose • Questioning faith beliefs

APPENDIX B
DEVELOPMENTAL STAGES OF CHILDREN AND HOW THEY DEAL WITH GRIEF
(From: www.kchospice.org) [2]

AGES 3 TO 5

- Don't understand "forever." Death is seen as temporary or reversible.
- Separation caused by illness is particularly frightening.
- Need reassurance that their emotions are normal and okay.
- "Magical thinking" is common—may believe their thoughts or actions are connected to illness or death.

AGES 6 TO 9

- Begin to understand that death is final, but think it only happens to other people.
- Very curious about illness and want details about physical changes that occur.
- Think illness is a scary creature or person who takes people away.
- Might fear that death is contagious.
- May continue to believe that their thoughts cause events.
- Worry harm might come to the caregivers—what will happen if those who care for them become sick.

AGES 9 TO 12

- Many have experienced the death of a relative or, more often, the loss of a pet.
- Know death is final and comes to all plants and animals.
- May be extremely interested in the physical process of dying, but still see death as distant from themselves.
- Worry about the effects the loss will have on their immediate future.

TEENS

- Forging their own identities—most do so by pushing their parents away and that is normal.
- The death of a parent can cause confusion and guilt.
- Death is fascinating, frightening and particularly threatening for adolescents.
- Don't like anything that makes them feel different from their peers.
- Losses may make teens feel more childlike and dependent, but may feel required to step into an adult role.

RECOMMENDED RESOURCES

CAMPS:

Camp Erin and Camp Mariposa (for children)

A yearly camp open to children and teens, ages 6 to 17, who have experienced the death of someone close to them. It is a free camp provided by the "The Moyer Foundation." The Foundation created and supports both signature programs.

My youngest son attended two summers and my daughter attended one. They met other kids from different states, so please take advantage of this opportunity even if you have to drive out of your state. Go to kchinfo@kchospice.org or www.kchcamps.org or call (816)363-2600, Monday – Friday 8:00 a.m. to 5:00 p.m. Central time.

Camp Carousel – Kansas City Hospice & Palliative Care (for families)

Camp Carousel is a special weekend retreat for grieving families with school-aged children and teens dealing with the loss of a loved one. The camp is located within an hour drive of the Kansas City metro; however, accepts families from surrounding states.

Go to www.kansascityhospice.org or call (816)363-2600, Monday – Friday 8:00 a.m. to 5:00 p.m. Central time.

ADDITIONAL GRIEF SUPPORT

SOLACE HOUSE

A center for grieving children, individuals, and families offering group and individual counseling. Solace House is part of Kansas City Hospice and Palliative Care. (913) 341-0318; www. solacehouse.org

(If you do not live in the Kansas City metro area, check with Hospice & Palliative Care—in your area to see if grief counseling or groups are offered.)

VIOLENT CRIME VICTIM SERVICES

253-383-5254 | www.vcvs.org

Area hospitals and local churches often provide grief support groups.

ESSENTIAL OILS:

If you could like more information on essential oils like: how to use them, what oils work best for promoting sleep and a calm environment, please email: shawnamertel@gmail.com.

ENDNOTES

CHAPTER ONE

1. Scientific American; *Mind*, published September 1,2015 by Jessica Schmerler

CHAPTER THREE

1. Lee, Steve. "Emotional Shock: How to Trip Back to Reality." Today's Therapist, May 9, 2017. July 28, 2019. www.todaystherapist.net/emotioal-shock/

2. Mercy Me. "Almost there." *I Can Only Imagine,* INO Records, 2001.\

CHAPTER FOUR

1. Colbert,M.D., Don. *Deadly Emotions.* Thomas Nelson Publishers, 2013, Introduction page x,xi, xii, and chapter 1, page 9.
2. Colbert, M.D., Don, *Deadly Emotions.* Thomas Nelson Publishers, 2013.
3. Hill, Napoleon. Editor, Melvin Powers. *Think and Grow Rich.* Wilshire Book Company, 1937

4. https://www.poetryfoundation.org/poems/51642/invictus Retrieved on 7-22-19

CHAPTER SIX

1. https://www.brainyquote.com/quotes/washington_irving_149294 Retrieved on July 22, 2019

CHAPTER EIGHT

1. https://www.azquotes.com/quote/582990 Retrieved on July 22, 2019

CONCLUSION

1. https://tonyagnesi.com/2018/04/grief-the-price-we-pay-for-love/ Retrieved July 22, 2019

APPENDICES

1. https://www.kchospice.org/wp-content/uploads/2016/05/SP-Understanding-Grief.pdf

2. "Safe Passage: Talking to children and Teens about Illness or Death." KCHospice, https://www.kchospice.org/wp-content/uploads/2016/05/SP-Child-Teen.pdf

WORKS CITED

Colbert, Don M. D. *Deadly Emotions: Understand the Mind-body-spirit Connection That Can Heal or Destroy You.* Thomas Nelson Publishers, 2006. Print.

Chapman, Steven Curtis. "Cinderella." *Deeper Roots: Where the Bluegrass Grows,* SCSEE Music, 2019.

Hill, Napoleon. Editor, Melvin Powers. *Think and Grow Rich.* Wilshire Book Company, 1937

https://hospicefoundation.org/End-of-Life-Support-and-Resources/Grief-Support/Journey-s-Newsletterhttps://tonyagnesi.com/2018/04/grief-the-price-we-pay-for-love/

Retrieved July 22, 2019.

https://www.azquotes.com/quote/582990 Retrieved on July 22, 2019.

https://www.brainyquote.com/quotes/washington_irving_149294 Retrieved on July 22, 2019.

http://www.dictionary.com

https://www.kchospice.org/wp-content/uploads/2016/05/SP-Understanding-Grief.pdf

http://www.lifescript.com/health/centers/heart_health/related_conditions/shock.aspx

https://www.poetryfoundation.org/poems/51642/invictus Retrieved on 7-22-19

https://tonyagnesi.com/2018/04/grief-the-price-we-pay-for-love/ Retrieved July 22, 2019

Lee, Steve. "Emotional Shock: How to Trip Back to Reality." Todays Therapist, May 9, 2017. July 28, 2019. www.todaystherapist.net/emotioal-shock/

Mercy Me. "Almost there." *I Can Only Imagine,* INO Records, 2001.

Scientific American; *Mind,* published September 1, 2015 by Jessica Schmerler

Steps to Forgiveness handout. 1998. *Remuda Ranch*: Center for Anorexia and Bulimia. Jack Burden Road, Box 2481, Wickenburg, Arizona 85358.

The Holy Bible, New Living Translation, copyright 1996, 2004, 2015. Used by permission of Tyndale House Publishers, Wheaton, Illinois 60189. All rights reserved.

The Holy Bible, King James Version.

The Holy Bible, New King James Version, Copyright 1979, 1980, 1982 by Thomas Nelson, Inc. Used by permission. All rights reserved.

The Holy Bible, New International Version, copyright 1973, 1978, 1984 by the International Bible Society. Used by permission of Zondervan. All rights reserved.